Williamsburg Christmas

Williamsburg Christmas
The Story of Christmas Decoration in the Colonial Capital

LIBBEY HODGES OLIVER AND MARY MILEY THEOBALD
PHOTOGRAPHS BY ERIK KVALSVIK

HARRY N. ABRAMS, INC., PUBLISHERS
in association with the
COLONIAL WILLIAMSBURG FOUNDATION

Page 1: The grocer's shop sign takes on a whole new meaning with this lighthearted Christmas treatment.

Page 2: A newel post is embellished with pinecones and yarrow and is accented with one large pomegranate.

Page 3: The backyards of Williamsburg offer simple views of the colonial capital in its Christmas finery.

Pages 4–5: As the sun sets, firelight from burning cressets casts a warm glow onto the brick facade of the Wythe House.

Page 6 top left: A five-card flush decorates this tavern window, highlighting the popularity of loo, whist, put, all-fours, and other colonial card games. Top right: Using looped strips of leather to proclaim his occupation, Williamsburg's shoemaker makes his Christmas decoration the way he makes his shoes, with sturdy materials to last the whole season long. Lower left: More like a freshly painted dollhouse in the woods than a storage house behind a city dwelling, this small outbuilding is home to at least three families of birds. Lower right: A split oak basket stuffed with cockscomb, yarrow, lotus pods, cotton bolls, and Fraser fir adds a welcoming flourish to a side gate.

Page 7 top left: The bright red berries of the hawthorn tree provided the colonists with winter color and the birds with winter food. Top right: The pattern of rubbed bricks surrounding the front entranceway call attention to the door and its Christmas splendor. Lower left: At Josiah Chowning's, the tavern theme is reflected in the wreath: oranges, lemons, and cinnamon are ingredients for a fine bowl of punch, and the tin mugs will see it down. Lower right: The crossed wooden spoons at the side of this basket emphasize the building's original function as a kitchen.

Page 8: "Above stairs" at the Wythe House, all is ready for the holiday guests.

Page 9: Inside the dining room bowfat—today restored to its original glazed green after extensive paint analysis—are some of the household's finest possessions.

Pages 10–11: On a cold December evening, candles and lanterns shine a cheerful welcome.

Editor: HOWARD W. REEVES
Editorial Assistant: LIA RONNEN
Designer: DARILYN LOWE CARNES

Library of Congress Cataloging-in-Publication Data
Oliver, Libbey Hodges.
    A Williamsburg Christmas / Libbey Hodges Oliver
and Mary Miley Theobald ; photographs by Erik Kvalsvik.
        p.   cm.
    Includes bibliographical references and index.
    ISBN 0–8109–4551–7
    1. Williamsburg (Va.)—Social life and customs.
2. Christmas decorations—Virginia—Williamsburg—
History. 3. Christmas—Virginia—Williamsburg—History.
I. Theobald, Mary Miley, 1952 – .   II. Kvalsvik, Erik.
III. Title.
F234.W7045   1999
975.5'4254—dc21   98–53974

Food styling on pages 72, 81, and 85 by Susan Bond
    Foresman
Drawings on pages 120–25 by Louis Luedtke © Colonial
    Williamsburg Foundation
Text and original photographs copyright © 1999 Harry
    N. Abrams, Inc.
All photographs by Erik Kvalsvik except selected photographs (pages 22, 23, 37, 42, 50, and 89) and
    archival material (pages 20, 27, 54, 55, and 76) copyright © 1999 Colonial Williamsburg Foundation.
Additional copyrights are indicated on their respective
    pages.
Published in 1999 by Harry N. Abrams, Incorporated,
    New York

Printed and bound in Japan

 Harry N. Abrams, Inc.
100 Fifth Avenue
New York, N.Y. 10011
www.abramsbooks.com

Contents

Prologue

Some say the origin of the single candle in the window harks back to an old European legend about welcoming the Christ child on a cold night, but in colonial Virginia, the practice was linked to the celebration of a royal milestone or the commemoration of a great military victory.

A WILLIAMSBURG CHRISTMAS. THE IMAGE PULLS AT THE MIND. CANDLES FLICKERING a welcome from the windowsills. Colorful fruits circling a fragrant evergreen wreath fastened above the door knocker. Inside, the Yule log sends a noisy shower of sparks onto the hearth and the scent of gingerbread fills the room. Boughs of holly deck the halls—and the tables, banisters, and doorways—and ivy tendrils drape the fireplace mantel. An apple pyramid crowned with a pineapple presides over a groaning board of Christmas feast. The memories of a traditional Williamsburg Christmas linger long after the wintery holidays have melted into spring.

OPPOSITE:
Gathering woodland greenery and decking the halls were among the many ancient Yuletide traditions that crossed the Atlantic.

Decorating for Christmas in the Williamsburg style has become as American as apple cones. Ever since the first official Colonial Williamsburg Christmas in 1935, visitors have thronged to the colonial capital to admire the decorations—taking notes, making sketches, posing questions, snapping photographs—in order to bring a little of Williamsburg home with them. For decades, magazines have featured the candlelit town with its handcrafted decorations, television crews have filmed the colonial wonderland, and department stores across the country have hosted sessions on Christmas decorating in the traditional Williamsburg style.

The decorating that began in Williamsburg in the depths of the Great Depression sparked a resurgence of interest in natural materials and homemade decorations that has spread across the country. Today, entire neighborhoods from Maine to California are aglow with a single candle in every window. Fruited wreaths hang as comfortably on doors of Texas homes as they do on Florida condominiums or Minnesota farmhouses. There is a Williamsburg Christmas block in Brooklyn, New York, and an entire neighborhood in Ohio that you might mistake for Virginia's colonial capital were you to walk its streets on a cold December night.

This is the story of the origins of Williamsburg's unique Christmas decorating style, how it evolved over the decades, and how it continues to adapt to the times.

The hospitality of the season becomes quite tangible in the back parlor of the home of Thomas Everard, onetime mayor of Williamsburg. Coffee is set for a gathering of gentlemen.

CHAPTER ONE

Christmas in Colonial Times

*"I hope you have spent the Christmas chearfully & merrily . . .
may each succeeding one be happier than the last! . . . Ps I had
almost forgot to tell you that my Fanny begs your Acceptance of a
pair of silk Stockings for a Christmas Box."*

—Letter to St. George Tucker, studying at the College of William and Mary, January 4, 1773

The height of the social season in colonial Virginia ran from Christmas to Twelfth Night. In this agricultural society, winters were a time of rest: Harvests had been gathered, and spring planting was still months away. Tidewater Virginia is blessed with mild winters, making travel by horse, carriage, or small boat quite manageable. Long visits lasting for weeks or even months were not uncommon among the Virginia gentry.

The holidays were more for adults than for children. For gentry families, Christmas Day involved a visit to church if one were near, followed by a sumptuous feast with an astonishing array of food and spirits. December was the time of year for slaughtering so there was fresh meat on the table

In England, servants and apprentices followed the ancient Roman tradition of collecting year-end tips in a clay "Christmas box."

OPPOSITE:
Bruton Parish Church was the only church in Williamsburg and was arguably the most important church in colonial Virginia. On Christmas Day, worshipers might have included the royal governor and his family, students from the College of William and Mary, townspeople, and outlying farmers and planters. The church has been in continual use since 1715.

as well as seafood from the nearby Chesapeake Bay and preserved fruits and vegetables, wines, and rum punches. Servants and slaves customarily received a portion of rum or other liquor and some time off from work; tutors gave their young charges a break from their studies. Small gifts or coins might come to servants, slaves, apprentices, or tradesmen in the English "Christmas box" tradition that would later evolve into the exchange of presents. Guns were fired into the air on Christmas Day and again to "shoot in the New Year," but most of the traditions we treasure—Christmas trees, Santa Claus, presents, Nativity scenes, elaborate decorations, Christmas cards, and the *Nutcracker* ballet—were as yet unknown.

"After Breakfast, we all retired into the Dancing-Room. . . . There were several Minuets danced with great ease and propriety; after which the whole company Joined in country-dances, and it was indeed beautiful to admiration, to see such a number of young persons, set off by dress to the best Advantage, moving easily, to the sound of well performed Music, and with perfect regularity, tho' apparently in the utmost Disorder—The Dance continued til two, we dined at half after three—soon after Dinner we repaired to the Dancing-Room again . . . [until] it grew too dark to dance."

—Philip Vickers Fithian, December 1773

The days preceding and following December 25 were highlighted by feasts, fox hunts, music and dancing, songs, games, and more feasts. As musicians played, Virginians danced minuets, country-dances, and the popular Sir Roger de Coverley, which came to be called the Virginia reel. It was a favorite time for weddings since so many people were gathered together in a celebratory mood. George Washington married the young widow Martha Dandridge Custis during the Christmas season at her home near Williamsburg. On a New Year's Day several years later, Martha Wayles Skelton wed Thomas Jefferson.

Genteel young ladies and gentlemen were expected to learn how to sing and dance and to play the harpsichord, violin, recorder, guitar, or other instrument at impromptu musical performances. Thomas Jefferson was one Virginian with a self-described passion for music, in particular the violin. During his Christmas break from studies in 1759, he played duets with another law student by the name of Patrick Henry. By all accounts, young Jefferson played well—well enough, at least, to be invited by Governor Francis Fauquier to perform at the Governor's Palace.

ABOVE AND OPPOSITE:

Winter weddings were popular in Virginia, especially during the days between Christmas and New Year's. In the colonial period and the early federal years, the marriage ceremony almost always took place in the bride's home and was followed by a supper party as elaborate as the family could afford. When William Wirt attended a Williamsburg wedding in 1806, he described the supper table decorations to his wife in a letter. "It was near twelve when it came to my turn to see the show. And a very superb one it was, I assure you. The tree in the centre cake was more simply elegant than anything of the kind I remember to have seen. It was near four foot high: the cake itself, the pedestal, had a rich—very rich—fringe of white paper surrounding it: the leaves, baskets, garlands, etc., etc., were all very naturally done in white paper, not touched with the pencil, and the baskets were rarely ornamented with silver spangles. At the ends of the tables were two lofty pyramids of jellies, syllabubs, ice creams, etc.—the pyramids were connected with the tree in the centre cake by pure white paper chains, very prettily cut, hanging in light and delicate festoons, and ornamented with paper bow-knots. Between the centre cake and each pyramid was another large cake made for use; then there was a profusion of meats, cheese-cakes, fruits, etc."

At the Market Square Tavern a pair of fruit plaques gives credence to the owner's boast of "The Best Accommodations." White pine and magnolia leaves provide the base for the lady apples, yarrow, cayenne peppers, boxwood, pineapples, cedar with berries, and goldenrod.

OPPOSITE:
Established about 1717, the Raleigh's reputation as the foremost of Williamsburg's taverns went unchallenged throughout the eighteenth century. A center for business and political gatherings, especially during the months directly preceding the Revolution, the Raleigh was also the site of countless balls, dinners, lectures, and concerts. Ladies, while welcome at these private social functions, were seldom seen in the taproom or the billiards room.

"Nothing is now to be heard of in conversation," marveled Philip Fithian on December 18, 1773, "but the Balls, the Fox-hunts, the fine entertainments, and the good fellowship, which are to be exhibited at the approaching Christmas." As tutor to one of colonial Virginia's wealthiest families, Fithian would experience a holiday more lavish than most. Common folk—the "middling sort"—participated in such entertainments on a more modest scale or not at all.

Traditions were very different to the north. New England's Puritan heritage meant that Christmas was not celebrated during colonial times. In fact, it was illegal in some colonies to observe the day at all, even in church. Massachusetts passed a law in 1659 warning that "whosoever shall be found observing any such day as Christmas, either by forbearing of labor, feasting, or any other way . . . shall pay for every such offence five shillings." Later, imprisonment and whipping were added. In Connecticut, even making mince pie was prohibited. With the passage of time, pressure from London caused these laws to be repealed, but few in New England recognized Christmas Day and even fewer marked it with any form of celebration until well into the nineteenth century.

However, depicting the Puritans as the Grinch who stole Christmas is far too simple. They were not dour workaholics bent on smothering the smallest breath of gaiety out of daily life; they had good reason to try to legislate Christmas out of existence. For centuries, Christmas in England had been celebrated in ways we would consider shockingly inappropriate today. The holiday had become little more than an excuse for riotous disorder, gambling,

OPPOSITE AND ABOVE:

In 1721, the Puritan minister Cotton Mather preached against the evils of Christmas celebration: "The Feast of Christ's Nativity is spent in Reveling, Dicing, Carding, Masking, and in all Licentious Liberty . . . by Mad Mirth, by long Eating, by hard Drinking, by Lewd Gaming, by rude Reveling." Note in the eighteenth-century print above the holly sprigs in the windowpanes that are echoed in the billiards room of the Raleigh Tavern.

wantonness, and dangerous drunken revelry—as though, many said, it were some heathenish feast of Saturn or Bacchus. The Puritans would have none of it.

In fairness, they were not alone in their disapproval of Christmas. Presbyterians, Methodists, Baptists, Congregationalists, Mennonites, Amish, and Quakers were generally in accord with the underlying desire to abolish all remnants of pagan and Roman Catholic ritual. But Virginia's established church was Anglican, and it had no thought of stamping out Christmas tradition.

ABOVE AND OPPOSITE:
A bounty of woodland berries and greens is brought to Bruton Parish each Christmas Eve in accordance with the old English custom known as "the sticking of the Church." Symmetrical arrangements of magnolia, pine, holly, pinecones, and nandina berries flank the altar. In the right foreground is the advent wreath—one candle is lit on each of the four Sundays before Christmas.

Christmas Decorations in the Colonial Period

"Against the Feast of Christmas, every mans house, as also their parish Churches, were decked with Holm [live oak], Ivy, Bayes, and whatsoever the season of the yeere aforded to be greene. The Conduits and Standards in the streetes were, likewise, garnished."

—*John Stow,* The Survey of London, *1618*

In England and in Virginia, Christmas decorations were a common sight inside churches. The approach of the holiday was an excuse to sweep the church clean, clear out the dust and cobwebs, and carry in the boughs of greenery. Garlands of holly, ivy, mountain laurel, and mistletoe dangled from the church walls, encircled pillars, and clung to second-story gallery railings, freshening the sanctuary with their clean, woodsy scent. Peter Kalm, a Swedish botanist who visited Philadelphia at Christmastime in 1749, wrote that "Pews and altar were decorated with branches of mountain laurel, whose leaves are green in winter time."

Private homes were similarly decorated. Evergreen garlands would be laced through rail-

The spare bedrooms of the George Wythe House are decorated for Christmas as if relatives have come to town for a holiday visit. The boldly colored wallpapers are recent additions to the Wythe House, reproduced especially for the site after research revealed that the walls had once been so fashionably covered. The new furnishings bring this elegant home closer to its original eighteenth-century appearance.

*"From every hedge is plucked by eager hands
The holly-branch with prickly leaves replete,
And fraught with berries of a crimson hue;
Which torn asunder from its parent trunk,
Is straightway taken to the neighboring towns;
Where windows, mantels, candlesticks, and shelves,
Quarts, pints, decanters, pipkins, basins, jugs,
And other articles of household-ware,
The verdant garb confess."*

—London, 1859

ings and banisters or across mantels, twigs of holly wedged into the wooden muntins of each windowpane, bouquets of fresh-picked greenery arranged in vases, and clusters of holly stuck behind picture frames or mirrors. Sometimes dried lavender, rose petals, rosemary, bay, and other sweet-scented herbs were scattered about for the sake of their pleasing aroma.

Christmas preparations of all sorts fell largely within the woman's sphere. Indeed, references linking women to Christmas decorations go back at least as far as the 1500s when, in one English poem, women are urged to "deck," or decorate, their houses for the holiday: "Get Iuye [ivy] and hull [holly], woman deck vp thyne house." Many American prints from the nineteenth century depict women buying holly boughs and other greenery at the market and hanging garlands in their parlors.

Perhaps decking the halls was an inevitable reaction to the bleak days of winter. After all, who would *not* think of bringing fresh-smelling evergreens indoors to cheer up the house and remind everyone that spring would come again.

Early colonists found Virginia's winter greenery somewhat different from what they were accustomed to back home. Native plant materials readily available in the Tidewater region included the familiar holly, pine, and mistletoe as well as the less familiar magnolia, ground pine, and mountain laurel. Mistletoe was not easy to gather. This parasite grows high in the tops of hardwood trees, often too high for climbing. It becomes visible only in the winter when deciduous leaves have fallen from the host tree, exposing the evergreen mistletoe at precisely

Originally used to ward off the foul odors thought to cause disease, the pomander had lost its magic by the eighteenth century and evolved into something valued more for its pleasant scent than its curative properties.

OPPOSITE:
The firing of "Christmas guns" was a colonial custom that continues in rural Virginia to the present day. Philip Fithian, tutor to the Carter children at Nomini Hall, noted in his journal, "I was waked this morning [December 25, 1773] by Guns fired all round the House."

Pomanders

To make pomanders, use a nail or skewer to punch holes in a lemon, lime, apple, or orange; stick the stems of whole cloves into the holes until the entire surface of the fruit is covered. In a bowl, mix ¼ cup cinnamon, ¼ cup powdered orris root, ¼ cup ground cloves, 2 T nutmeg, and 2 T allspice. Roll the fruit in the spice mixture and let it dry in the bowl for several weeks, turning the fruit daily until it shrinks and hardens. Dust off the spices.

the right moment of the year. Shooting down mistletoe became a popular holiday sport for boys.

The many rivers and small ports in the colony allowed Virginians to enjoy the luxury of fresh fruits out of season. Colonial merchants imported fruit from other British colonies in the West Indies: pineapples from the Bahamas and oranges, lemons, and limes by the barrel from Antigua, Barbados, Jamaica, Bermuda, Nevis, and the Bahamas—and sometimes even from as far away as Portugal. Fresh apples and bright red cranberries came from the New England colonies. Costly, rare, and much appreciated, fresh fruits added elegance to any table, especially to a Christmas feast.

Fresh fruit was far too precious to be used as decoration, as we do today. Any colonist hanging fruit on his front door in the middle of winter to rot or be devoured by squirrels would have been thought, at best, highly eccentric by his neighbors. In fact, there is no indication that any of Virginia's early colonists decorated the *outside* of their homes for Christmas at all.

But indoors the fireplaces were ablaze with hospitality for friends, family, and strangers alike. By the middle of the eighteenth century, tales of Virginia Christmas celebrations had traveled back to England, giving the colony a certain mystique later known as "Southern hospitality." The *London Magazine* extolled the virtues of a colonial Virginia Christmas in 1746: "All over the Colony, an universal Hospitality reigns, full Tables and open Doors, the kind Salute, the generous Detention . . . . Strangers are fought after with Greediness, as they pass the Country, to be invited."

CHAPTER TWO

Williamsburg Christmas Traditions

"The damsel donn'd her kirtle sheen;
The hall was dress'd with holly green,
Forth to the wood did merry-men go,
To gather in the mistletoe."

—*Sir Walter Scott,* Marmion, *1808*

An unusually large piece of fresh mistletoe hangs over the doorway that divides the Governor's Palace supper room from the ballroom.

OPPOSITE:
As the residence of His Majesty's representative, the Palace was designed and furnished as a tangible symbol of royal might.

When the Virginia capital moved to Richmond in 1780, the town of Williamsburg settled into relative insignificance. For the next century and a half, little in Williamsburg changed. Virginia's governor no longer lived at the Palace and Virginia's legislature no longer gathered in the Capitol building—indeed, both buildings were destroyed by fire—but the little town would not die. Williamsburg was still the county seat and home to the state's only public hospital and oldest college, and it clung to these remnants of its former glory throughout the turmoil of the Civil War and the poverty of Reconstruction. Ultimately, Williamsburg's very obscurity was what preserved it for future generations, for in this stagnant back-water, there was little reason to knock down old buildings and replace them with new ones.

During these quiet decades, the Christmas celebration grew to include several new "traditions." The open house of earlier days remained in vogue, as did the emphasis on parties, feasting, and drinking, but Santa Claus and table-top Christmas trees were gaining in popularity. Firecrackers replaced the shooting of guns—at least in urban areas. Instead of the traditional "Christmas box" tip to underlings, wrapped gifts passed from friend to friend and among family members. As the Victorian era progressed, Christmas became the focus of decorating extravagance.

Oddly enough, it was in Williamsburg, where change usually arrived rather later than

This sketch by German painter John Lewis Krimmel is the earliest known depiction of an American Christmas tree. He drew the scene while on a trip through Pennsylvania in either 1812 or 1819. Courtesy, The Winterthur Library: Joseph Downs Collection of Manuscripts and Printed Ephemera

elsewhere, that the earliest known Christmas tree in Virginia is found. As everyone knows, the decorated evergreen tree is a German tradition with roots in the pagan festivals of ancient Rome. The custom was carried to America with the cultural baggage of the German immigrants, and virtually all of the early references to Christmas trees in America have German connections. In that respect, the Williamsburg story is typical.

In 1842, Judge Nathaniel Beverley Tucker invited a young German-born professor at the College of William and Mary to share his family's Christmas celebration. No doubt feeling a bit homesick for his native land, Professor Charles Minnigerode asked the judge if he might prepare the children a little tree after the German custom. He brought a small evergreen

into the parlor and showed the Tucker children how to make simple decorations with bits of brightly colored paper. He fastened candle stubs to the ends of the branches with twisted pieces of wire, then finished by hanging a gilded star at the top.

Word of the Christmas tree spread quickly. There were several parties for neighborhood children, and some young cousins traveled all the way from Petersburg—a hard day's journey—to see this Yuletide creation. Enchanted, the Tucker family continued the Christmas tree tradition in the years to come, thus becoming the first non-German Americans known to have adopted this Old World tradition as their own. By the turn of the century, floor-to-ceiling trees had replaced the tabletop size, and one family in five had a decorated Christmas tree in its home.

The first Christmas tree in Williamsburg was created in 1842 by a German immigrant professor from the College of William and Mary. "He said his holiday wouldn't be complete without it," recalled Martha Vandergrift in the 1920s, "and he wanted Chick [her cousin] and me to see one for the first time. . . . We children danced and shouted for joy when those candles were lit one by one. We'd never seen anything in the world so beautiful! I've never had a merrier Christmas as that one—never, ever—and I've had ninety-five of 'em!" Every year Colonial Williamsburg commemorates this event by setting up a replica of that first tree in the same room where it first appeared in the St. George Tucker House.

The First Colonial Williamsburg Christmas

"These dear Virginians! They are not Americans at all. They are just old fashioned English folk. One keeps wondering what on earth they are doing here. This is old England, old England at its best and kindliest . . . how delighted Charles Dickens would be with these Virginians."

—The Bishop of Aberdeen, Scotland, 1927

Ever since colonial days, Christmas in the Old Dominion, as Virginia came to be known, has been painted with sentimental colors. Visitors from Europe found its celebrations charming; Americans from other parts of the country copied its ways. Books and magazine articles about the holidays nearly always sketched an "Old Virginia" Christmas, a nostalgic look back at times and traditions that glowed all the more warmly with the passing of the years.

By Christmas 1934, the partially restored town of Williamsburg had been officially open to the public for only a few months. Curious visitors flocked to Virginia's colonial capital to see for themselves what the wealthy philanthropist John D. Rockefeller, Jr., had been doing for the past five years, stripping away the layers of time to reveal the forgotten face of eighteenth-century America. No one working at Colonial Williamsburg that year was expecting visitors over the holiday, yet a glance up and down the main street on Christmas Day showed that the town was far from empty. Visitors did come—they have been coming ever since—but on that first Christmas in restored Williamsburg, they saw precious little evidence of Christmas.

At one end of the street stood the College of William and Mary, silent, empty of students. Bright red electric lights shone from the windows of the Wren Building, newly restored with Rockefeller money. Along the Duke of Gloucester Street, which stretched precisely one mile between the college and the Capitol, someone had selected, quite randomly, ten live evergreens and decked them with bright strands of colored lights. That was all. A rather inauspicious start for what would soon sweep the country as "the Williamsburg-style Christmas."

Underwhelmed by the effort, Colonial Williamsburg President Kenneth Chorley directed that the colored-light Christmas trees be discontinued, electricity and Christmas trees being unknown to the Virginia colonists. Vowing that Christmas would not catch Williamsburg unprepared again, he instructed the research department to delve into the Yuletide celebrations of colonial times and find historical practices and modes of decoration that could be revived.

The Williamsburg research team discovered very little. Louise Fisher, who was in charge of putting fresh flowers in the four exhibition buildings, spent days poring over documents in the Library of Congress without finding much in the way of descriptive references to Christmas in Virginia. Diaries and letters from the colonial period had little to say about the holiday. Typical is one of George Washington's Christmas Day journal entries in which he noted laconically, "Went to Pohick church and returned to dinner."

"With holly and ivy so green and so gay,
We deck up our houses as fresh as the day."

—Poor Robin's Almanack, *1695*

In Williamsburg, windowsill decorations are often set in the corner to prevent the greens from blocking the candlelight when darkness falls.

With no eighteenth-century Virginia sources to show exactly how colonists decorated for Christmas, Mrs. Fisher and her successors looked to English prints and documents of the period on the assumption that transplanted Englishmen would continue to follow English tradition, decorating their homes and churches with whatever winter greenery was plentiful. This evidence became the foundation for the historical creations that have been displayed in Williamsburg ever since.

Try as they might, Williamsburg's historians could not unearth much evidence for colonial Christmas decorations out-of-doors. The Virginia colonists may have strewn their homes with greens and feasted and danced until the wee hours of the morning, but it seemed they did not decorate the outside of their houses in any way. Nor, of course, did they set up Christmas trees, string lights, display crèche scenes, or participate in any of the other visuals so solidly fixed in the hearts of modern American celebrants.

To strip the town bare of exterior decorations in the name of historical authenticity was clearly going to be unpopular. For the many families living inside the boundaries of Williamsburg's Historic Area and for the thousands of holiday visitors, a strict colonial Christmas would seem like no Christmas at all.

The Reverend Dr. W. A. R. Goodwin, rector of Bruton Parish and the inspiration for the restoration of old Williamsburg, spoke for many. Williamsburg was not a museum, he said, but a living town whose residents could not be expected to forgo their own holiday traditions for the sake of historical accuracy. Clearly, there would have to be some compromise between authenticity and modern expectations.

There was. And care was taken to ensure that the public was not given any mistaken impressions. Christmas in Williamsburg was never meant to be a re-creation of the eighteenth-century version. Visitors would see an old-fashioned Christmas, a traditional Christmas, a homemade Christmas based on elements from America's past.

"Light Your Candles!"

"The Palace or Governor's House has the ornamental addition of a good cupola or lanthorn, illuminated with most of the town, upon birth-nights, and other nights of occasional rejoicings."

—Hugh Jones, 1724

Newly restored Williamsburg needed some special outdoor Christmas decorations, and President Chorley was determined not to succumb to garish strings of colored lights. He heard what sounded like a good old-fashioned idea from Boston's Beacon Hill: the placement of a single lighted candle in every window.

The colonists called it "illumination" and the practice was historically correct—illuminations did occur during the colonial era, often in conjunction with fireworks and bonfires to commemorate a royal milestone or important battle. Usually, a single candle was placed in the cupolas of public buildings and in the windows of gentlemen's homes. When in 1702 the College of William and Mary was illuminated for ceremonies honoring the ascension of Queen Anne, the windows of the Wren Building "were set with a double row of candles." Although illumination had not historically been associated with Christmas, it appealed to most people and was approved for the next year.

The Williamsburg plan called for candlelight to flicker from the windows of the Governor's Palace, the Capitol, the Raleigh Tavern, and the Paradise House—the only exhibition buildings open to the public in those first years—from 5 P.M. until 10 P.M. between Christmas Eve and

The Wren Building, built shortly after the College of William and Mary received its royal charter in 1693, is the oldest academic building still in use in America. Since 1940, white lights have illuminated its facade at every Christmas.

Twilight marks the start of each night's illumination as residents of Historic Area houses move from room to room to light electric candles in every window and dormer. The Grissell Hay Lodging House, pictured here, is one of the oldest homes on Market Square.

OPPOSITE:

On a wintry evening in 1774, all of Williamsburg turned out to welcome Lady Dunmore, the governor's wife, to Virginia. Then, as now, windows throughout the town glowed warmly with candlelight. In spite of rising political tensions, Virginians still considered themselves British subjects, and the gracious Lady Dunmore became quite popular, especially after she chose to name her newborn daughter Virginia.

New Year's Eve. Mrs. Fisher would decorate the doors and windows of the Governor's Palace and the Raleigh Tavern with simple, fresh greenery. The cost of the entire effort—fifty dollars.

With visions of charred ruins dancing in his head, a nervous Dr. Goodwin urged that each candlestick be placed in a dish of water. Four custodians were paid one dollar apiece each night to light and extinguish the candles in the exhibition buildings and to stand guard against accidental fires.

Williamsburg's entire population was encouraged to participate through an announcement in the *Virginia Gazette.* The response was tepid. Candles in every window needed to be replaced daily—no insignificant expense during the depths of the Depression—and it was necessary to stay at home while they burned. Most townspeople ignored the request.

Persuading Williamsburg residents to participate in what was termed "White Lighting" also would require quenching their fear of fire. A three-way compromise between historical authenticity, safety, and modern celebration appeared on the scene in the form of electrified candles with white light bulbs. By 1940, one-quarter of the town's homes were decorated with electrified candles. Strings of colored lights were on their way out.

One of those who clung to recent custom was John Stewart Bryan, president of the College of William and Mary and a devotee of colored lights. Influenced, perhaps, by the Victorian penchant for red Christmas candles, he had for years decked the halls of the Wren Building—or at least its windows—with glowing red electric lights. Mrs. Fisher had been

dropping what she thought were tactful hints for some time, hoping to coax the college into the white candlelight fold, but to no avail. At last, in 1940, President Bryan graciously acceded to the Restoration's request for white lights.

With every passing year, more residents chose to light their private homes with candles. Williamsburg merchants stocked up on the heretofore unusual faux candles and found their inventories quickly depleted, not by local residents but by visitors from out of town. Quite unexpectedly, the custom was spreading beyond the Historic Area.

During World War II, with American factories wholly geared to military needs, nonessential consumer goods such as electrified candles became impossible to buy. Blackouts made them impossible to use. (The only other time that Williamsburg's candlelighting had to be canceled was during the 1973 energy crisis.) Not until after the war were the buildings lit again, this time with a new sort of flame-shaped bulb that looked very much like a real candle. Today, Colonial Williamsburg has begun using an improved battery-powered candle that its proponents claim is safer still.

By the late forties, a ceremony had evolved around the first night of the lighting of the candles. Originally called "White Lighting," it became more elaborate and drew larger crowds with each passing year. Church and college bells signaled the start of the ceremony. The Singing Candles—caroling schoolchildren holding lighted

Wrought-iron cressets date back to the ancient Greeks. In the colonial South, lightwood, a resinous pine easily kindled, was the common fuel. When twilight comes early and visitors stay late, Williamsburg's cressets light the walkways as well as any modern street lamp.

tapers—performed. A costumed night watch carrying a flaming torch led the procession through the streets of Williamsburg, followed by the Fife and Drum Corps, the Militia, and hundreds of eager visitors. Flaming cressets lit the way. At every house the night watch paused and called out in a booming voice to its occupant, "Light your candles!" At the command, the candles in the house would begin to glow, one by one, until every window was lit and the procession continued on its way.

In 1959, the White Lighting ceremony changed its name to the Grand Illumination. The event had already begun a steady march backward on the calendar from its original date of Christmas Eve. In order to accommodate the increasing throngs that came to Williamsburg in December to see the lights and decorations, a longer season was necessary. Grand Illumination now falls during the first week of December.

The result was an ever-widening circle of public awareness. Tens of thousands of people visiting the colonial capital each December borrowed the custom for their own. As candlelighting spread westward across the country, stores everywhere responded to public demand for this inexpensive, old-fashioned, elegant form of holiday decoration.

Today, it is not unusual to see entire neighborhoods aglow with a candle in every window. In some regions, the practice is so entrenched that homebuilders wire new houses so that all the candles turn on and off with one flick of a switch. The 1935 experiment of a different sort of Christmas light has become one of the most popular ways Americans decorate for the holidays.

Fireworks

"When it was to begin the Governor asked if they were ready. They answered: 'Yes.' Then he commanded them to set off the fireworks."

—*Francis Louis Michel, Williamsburg, 1702*

Historical purists approved of the bonfires, which started in the late thirties, and the fireworks, the first of which shot up from behind the Williamsburg Inn on Christmas Day in 1940. Thereafter, fireworks and bonfires were a regular part of Williamsburg's ever-more-elaborate Christmas celebration package.

Fireworks, like illuminations, were not historically associated with Christmas. They were, however, popular eighteenth-century attractions usually linked to a monarch's birthday or the commemoration of a great military victory. Records show that in 1702, the citizens of Williamsburg enjoyed a spectacular fireworks display in honor of Queen Anne's ascension to the throne, including on-ground "set pieces" as well as rockets. All did not go as planned. Francis Louis Michel, a Swiss traveler, described the scene: "A firemaster was considered the most expert and boasted of his skill. But the result showed that he did not succeed in gaining much honor. In order to preserve his reputation he acted as if the fire had fallen unintentionally into the fireworks, for he blew up everything at once in a great blaze and smoke. As there were all kinds of fireworks, many and large rockets, he like others had to run and he had his clothes burnt."

At that point, the royal governor himself stepped in to supervise the remaining fireworks. When everything was in place, he gave the order to begin: "This was done with a reversed rocket, which was to pass along a string to an arbor, where prominent ladies were seated, but it got stuck half way and exploded. Two stars were to be made to revolve through the fireworks, but they succeeded no better than with the rockets. In short, nothing was successful, the rockets also refused to fly up, but fell down archlike so that it was not worth while seeing. Most of the people, however, had never seen such things and praised them highly."

In 1957, as part of the special celebration of nearby Jamestown's 350th anniversary, Colonial Williamsburg fired its first set pieces in a show on Market Square. They included pictoral renditions of Captain John Smith, the three Jamestown ships, and—perhaps to make amends for the 1702 fiasco—a sparkling star. Since then, fireworks, both set and aerial, have been an integral part of a Williamsburg Christmas.

OPPOSITE:
From the seventeenth century onward, occasions of national rejoicing were often celebrated with fireworks. These early displays were primitive by modern standards, devoid of color until the nineteenth century, but were exceedingly popular nonetheless. Colonial Williamsburg revived the fireworks custom in 1940, thus linking fireworks—for the first time—to the Christmas celebration.

The art of della Robbia enjoyed a modest revival in the early twentieth century. His enameled terra-cottas, such as this Madonna and Child, were often surrounded by garlands of fruit and foliage. Courtesy, Virginia Museum of Fine Arts, Richmond. Mrs. Alfred I. DuPont Fund. Photo: Katherine Wetzel. ©Virginia Museum of Fine Arts.

Wreaths and Swags

"The days before Christmas were spent in cutting cedar pine boughs and holly for decoration . . . tie[ing] long lengths of string to make garlands . . . . All windows had holly wreaths, and the pictures had sprigs of holly . . . ."

—*Memoirs of Nancy Keene Perkins Lancaster, ca. 1905–15*

Before long, Mrs. Fisher, the "flower lady," felt impelled to move beyond the plain green wreaths she had first used. Inspired by the renewed interest in fifteenth-century Italian sculptor Luca della Robbia (who had no stylistic influence on eighteenth-century English or American decorative arts) and Englishman Grinling Gibbons (who did), she began affixing fresh fruit to the wreaths. To keep within the

This della Robbia-style wreath is garnished with a peculiar-looking, inedible fruit known as the Osage orange, called bois d'arc *or hedge apple in some parts of the country. Its chief virtue, aside from its curious appearance, is its longevity. When gathered for decoration, it can last for weeks.*

boundaries of colonial American history, she used Robert Furber's prints and other period documentation to select only those fruits or plants known to have been available to colonial Virginians. And she hung them on the outside of the front doors of the exhibition buildings.

The public loved them. Within a few years, Mrs. Fisher's "della Robbia wreaths" were a stylistic sensation. More wreaths and swags were needed for other houses and exhibition buildings, and soon more women were trained to help with the arrangements. National home and garden magazines featured articles on the Williamsburg decorations and printed directions for those who wished to make their own. Everyone, it seemed, wanted a Williamsburg wreath for the front door and an old-fashioned Williamsburg Christmas inside.

1. Royal purple Auricula.
African white flower'd Heath.
3. Pansies or Hearts ease.
4. White Corn Marigold.
5. Strawberry daisie.
6. Cape Marigold.
7. Shining leav'd Laurustinus.
8. Marvel du Mond Auricula.
9. Red spring Cyclamen.

10. White Cyclamen.
11. Yellow Ficoides.
12. Yellow round Eternal.
13. Christmas flower.
14. Winter white Primrose.
15. Gentianella.
16. Yellow Corn Marigold.
17. Scarlet Geranium.
18. Canary Pellitory.

DECEMBER

19. Valerianella.
20. Winter double Crowfoot.
21. Stript leav'd Geranium.
22. Cape Marigold white within.
23. St. Peters Shrub.
24. Mountain Avens.
25. Single purple Anemone.
26. Sage & Rosemary tree.
27. Winter wall flower.

28. Winter flowering Pear.
29. Lavendercow'd Groundsel tree.
30. Scarlet African Aloe, with
Pine apple Leaves.
31. Spanish Virgins bower.
32. Glastenbury thorne.
33. Humble plant.
34. Casella.
35. Monthly rose bud.
36. Trifoli African golden knot.

From the Collection of Robt Furber Gardiner at Kensington. 1730.   Engrav'd by H. Fletcher.

OPPOSITE AND ABOVE:

In 1730, English nurseryman Robert Furber published an unusually artistic catalogue: In twelve prints, he depicted four hundred varieties of flowers grouped by the month in which they bloom. The series proved so popular that he followed it two years later with "Twelve Months of Fruits," this time grouping the specimens according to the month in which they ripen. Colonial Williamsburg flower arrangers and Christmas decorators use these colorful prints to guide them in the selection of appropriate winter fruits and flowers.

CHAPTER THREE

Deck the Doors

*"The Rooms were embower'd with Holly, Ivy, Cyprus,
Bays, Laurel and Mistletoe, and a bouncing Christmas
Log in the Chimney, glowing like the Cheeks of a
Country Milkmaid . . . ."*

—*F. Roberts,* Round about Our Coal-Fire, *ca. 1740*

T hose fruit-bedecked wreaths that decorate America's front doors did not originate in Williamsburg, nor did they begin during colonial times. No matter. Everyone from Augusta to Albuquerque calls them "Colonial Williamsburg door decorations" anyway, and millions of people have visited the Historic Area during the Christmas season for the sole purpose of admiring them.

The custom of affixing fruits, vegetables, dried flowers, herbs, and other of nature's creations to basic Christmas forms such as wreaths, swags, and roping traces its roots to the early years of the twentieth century, a time when Christmas was growing in significance and the Colonial Revival movement was pulling decorative impulses back toward the eighteenth century.

Crossed earthenware pipes take the place of a ribbon bow on this attractive wreath. The use of ribbons in Historic Area Christmas decorations is discouraged as a Victorian ornamentation not suited to Colonial Revival style.

OPPOSITE:

The unicorn's horn at the left of the wreaths was a traditional apothecary's symbol. People in the Middle Ages considered powdered unicorn's horn an antidote for poison—by the eighteenth century such beliefs had faded.

"Of late years," explained the December 1926 issue of *House Beautiful,* "besides the staple wreaths of plain greens to which we have long been accustomed, the holiday's emblems have blossomed forth—or perhaps we should say fruited forth—with richness of color produced by the use of either natural or artificial fruit as an embellishment. This idea was undoubtedly suggested by the gorgeous Italian carvings and terra cottas of the Renaissance."

The magazine editor was referring to Luca della Robbia and his progeny, the family whose name has become synonymous with fruit and foliage garlands. One of the most significant artists of the Renaissance, della Robbia gained fame for his

The Benjamin Powell House door is decorated with shiny magnolia leaves and long sticks of cinnamon wedged between the fruit. The elaborate display shows up well against the dark Spanish brown color of the front door.

OPPOSITE:
The Coke-Garrett House, an amalgam of four eighteenth- and early-nineteenth-century buildings, was the residence and workplace of a Williamsburg goldsmith and tavern keeper. The stark simplicity of the bright red apple ring provides Christmas color; the pineapple adds a dash of holiday hospitality.

enameled, colored, terra-cotta creations, works of art he often framed with wreaths, fruits, and flowers. His timeless designs inspired many to create their own Christmas wreaths and swags; some even shellacked their fruit to imitate the shiny della Robbia glaze.

There is, however, another influence, one closer at hand: an Englishman with the improbable name of Grinling Gibbons. Gibbons produced ornamental wood carvings with festoons of fruit, flowers, and other bits of nature until his death in 1720. The most famous English sculptor of his time, he set the pattern for baroque interiors with his carvings in cathedrals and royal palaces and influenced English—and colonial—style.

The linking of fruited wreaths with Christmas seems to have started in America's wealthier homes during the early years of the twentieth century. To judge by the home and garden decorating magazines of the day, Christmas greenery was still largely an indoor phenomenon. Only rarely do the upscale publications show photographs of homes with simple outdoor holiday trim, and when they do, there is little more than a plain wreath on the front door. It was left to Colonial Williamsburg to popularize this sort of fruited decoration among the country's expanding postwar middle class and to bring the wreaths outside.

When Colonial Williamsburg began decorating for Christmas, the greenery consisted of a few plain wreaths and some running cedar to drape about the Governor's Palace and the Raleigh Tavern. But by 1939, Mrs. Fisher's fruited wreaths were attracting considerable comment and the "Williamsburg Christmas look" was

Pinecones and fluffy cotton bolls keep the pomegranates and oranges company on this large fir wreath at the Margaret Hunter Millinery Shop. This building's decoration is always one of the most photographed in town.

OPPOSITE:
Pine roping surrounds the double doorway of the George Davenport House, owned in the eighteenth century by a respected Williamsburg attorney. Fastened to the wreath are apples, oranges, dried okra pods, yarrow, and pinecones.

ABOVE:

The effect of sculptor Grinling Gibbons on Williamsburg Christmas decorations is evident in many of the exterior swags and garlands.

RIGHT:

Gibbons' artful arrangements of nuts, leaves, pods, fruits, and flowers inspired Williamsburg's first naturalistic decorations in the 1930s. Examples of his work continue to guide today's creations along an eighteenth-century path. Courtesy, Victoria and Albert Museum, ©V&A Picture Library

This house belonged to blacksmith James Anderson, hired by the Commonwealth of Virginia to clean and repair muskets, swords, and bayonets during the Revolutionary War. Among the materials incorporated into the green-and-gold color scheme are pineapples, green apples, lady apples, lotus pods, yarrow, cockscomb, and an Osage orange.

At the Elizabeth Carlos House, orange slices and honesty (or money plant) mix with pinecones on a pine backdrop. Evidence suggests that Elizabeth Carlos was a milliner and dressmaker who carried on her business from her home.

launched. Yet no matter how festive the exhibition buildings, the private homes that lined the streets of the restored town remained an anachronistic mixture of personal holiday preferences. The residents of Williamsburg would need some encouragement to abandon the modern trappings of Christmas for an old-fashioned look. A competition was the answer.

The first contest for house decorations took place in 1937. Rules were drawn up by the local garden club and awards presented at the bonfire on Market Square. To encourage participation, the Colonial Williamsburg Foundation provided basic cut greenery for free and awarded cash prizes.

Never mind that no one in the eighteenth

century would have tacked fresh fruit to his front door. The contest caught on at once. Many took it very seriously. Blue ribbons affixed to the houses proclaimed the winners (usually five to ten), and the public became so enamored of the contest that the "Christmas Decorations Tour" was inaugurated in 1969.

The decorating style adopted and adapted by Colonial Williamsburg in the early years of its Restoration spread across the country by means of continual publicity in home and garden magazines. Thousands of visitors fascinated by the imaginative decorations strolled the streets of Williamsburg, snapping pictures of their favorite creations to try back home. Visitor queries resulted in how-to books and videos,

ABOVE LEFT:
At the entrance to the Raleigh Tavern, twin wreaths made of fir and grapevine are decked with cardoon, strawflowers, and split trumpet vine pods; above the door are beauty berries, dock, and pokeberries. The tavern was named for Sir Walter Raleigh, the bold adventurer and favorite of Queen Elizabeth, who bestowed the name "Virginia" on his country's first North American colony in honor of the Virgin Queen.

ABOVE RIGHT:
Visitors who take the time to leave the main street and explore Williamsburg's backyard gardens are rewarded with the unexpected sight of outbuildings decorated with as much care as the main houses. Tucked away behind the Hartwell Perry Ordinary is its kitchen with a checkerboard pattern of lemons wedged into the door.

workshops, and television demonstrations until a virtual cottage industry of instruction and materials had sprung up. Soon professional florists across the country were helping the do-it-yourself market by supplying wire wreath frames wrapped with heavy green paper and stuffed with wet sphagnum moss. Today, Williamsburg Christmas decorating contests are held in neighborhoods, retirement communities, and apartment complexes all over the country.

The nature of the door decorations has changed noticeably over the past seventy years. Tastes have changed, of course—the pictorial themes so popular in the fifties and sixties are no longer in evidence—but it goes farther than that. Conservation concerns led to the elimination of running cedar and mountain laurel. After 1976, Colonial Williamsburg promoted the use of pine, always plentiful, as an alternative to what was becoming a wholesale destruction of native mountain laurel and holly for wreaths and roping. Authenticity concerns caused the banning of ribbon and bows (too Victorian), fake fruit, and any materials not available to eighteenth-century residents of Williamsburg such as poinsettias, pepper berries, and eucalyptus.

The gradual lengthening of the Williamsburg Christmas season from one week to six brought about a surge in the use of dried materials: Acorns, dried flowers, dried peppers, nuts, and cotton bolls did not have to be replenished every few days as did pears and lemons. "Freezing temperatures at night followed by the hot sun during the day can destroy some fruits faster than they can be replaced," explained one long-time Historic Area resident. Other residents have begun using newer tricks such as the floral

OPPOSITE FROM LEFT TO RIGHT:
With magnolia and boxwood as a base and fresh fruit arranged on top, this plaque attests to the importance of symmetry in colonial design.

In a tongue-in-cheek allusion to the eighteenth-century function of this outbuilding, white soap balls have been incorporated into the decorative scheme of this former laundry. Both the bright purple flowers and the small white ones that encircle the soap balls are dried globe amaranths. Acorn caps complete the picture.

Residents of the Charlton House created a dramatic dried arrangement using an unusual brown color scheme. Dried magnolia leaves, pinecones, and sweet bay magnolia pods form the base for the red-and-white accents of pomegranates and onions.

A golden ring of dried yarrow flowers surrounded by tiny bayberries is fastened to the weatherboards of the Golden Ball silversmith shop.

cage (a container holding wet floral foam) to prolong the life of fragile plant materials such as ivy.

In the 1970s, Williamsburg's outdoor decorations became more elaborate with the introduction of a wooden form shaped like an open fan and studded with headless nails upon which fruit was attached. Although not a new invention—directions for something similar were published in at least one Depression-era Christmas decorating guide—the apple fan was an immediate hit. Visitors asked for directions; magazines featured it in their Christmas issues.

The apple fan made its Williamsburg debut when a local couple, who worked for Colonial Williamsburg as a carpenter and an interior decorator, devised a wooden form studded with headless nails. They stuck a semicircular swath of apples on it, affixed a pineapple in the middle, then hoisted the whole thing above the doorway of their Historic Area home. It created a minor sensation.

OPPOSITE:
The first contest for house decoration took place in 1937. To encourage participation, Colonial Williamsburg provided workshops and basic cut greens for free and gave prizes, usually five to ten, for the best-decorated homes. This decoration at the Custis Tenement was a blue-ribbon winner.

The apple fan was a classic Colonial Revival idea. By using the balanced symmetry so typical of Georgian design and incorporating the architectural features of the original Williamsburg buildings, the apple fans lifted the della Robbia–inspired wreaths from the front door to the pediment or transom above. As was the case with wreaths and garlands, only fruits and natural materials available to the Virginia colonists (red and green apples, lemons, pineapples, magnolia leaves, and such) were permitted within the Historic Area.

More recently, those who live within the Historic Area have incorporated into their decorating scheme objects that relate to the original use of their building or to colonial times in general. A former tavern dangles reproduction playing cards in the windows; a wreath on the front door of an eighteenth-century kitchen is decorated with crossed wooden spoons and red-checked napkins. Clay pipes, pheasant feathers, oyster shells, tobacco twists, straw toys, blown eggshells, clay wig curlers, ribbon cockades, even earthenware bird bottles have seen decorative use in past years. Some residents who work in the historic trades seize the opportunity to personalize their decorations with evidence of their craft. A harness maker works braided leather into his windowsill swags, a baker fashions a fanciful bread wreath, a cabinetmaker incorporates wood shavings into his decorations, and a weaver highlights her holiday greenery with tassels of brightly dyed yarns. For those who can read the clues, these imaginative Christmas decorations tell a story about the old buildings and the manner of people who live and work there today.

OPPOSITE ABOVE:

Outside the Dubois Grocer Shop, even the birds celebrate Christmas. The decoration incorporates cayenne peppers, rose hips, and cotton bolls on a grapevine wreath that is looped around an earthenware bird bottle. Decades ago, when Williamsburg archaeologists first excavated fragments of an odd sort of earthenware jar, no one knew its purpose. When it was finally identified as a clay birdhouse, curators had it reproduced—much to the delight of the local avian population.

OPPOSITE BELOW:

This plaque makes a perfect decoration for the John Greenhow Store, where once again visitors to Williamsburg can buy the long-stemmed clay pipes so popular in colonial times. Oyster shells and pomegranates add Christmas colors.

ABOVE LEFT:

A colonial Christmas dinner would not be complete without shellfish and other seafood from the nearby rivers, bay, and ocean. Here, scallop shells decorate the wreath on the door of the Nelson-Galt House, one of the oldest buildings in Williamsburg. General Thomas Nelson, the eighteenth-century owner, was a signer of the Declaration of Independence.

ABOVE RIGHT:

In recent years, Historic Area residents have delighted in trying to incorporate meaningful objects into their Christmas decorations. At the Blue Bell Tavern, reproduction playing cards allude to one of the most popular pastimes in colonial Virginia.

CHAPTER FOUR

Groaning Boards

"At Christmas be mery, and thanke god of all:
and feast thy pore neighbours, the great and the small."

—*Thomas Tusser, 1577*

When it came to excessive eating and drinking during the Christmas season, Englishmen and colonial Virginians had much in common. A sumptuously spread Christmas table had long been a mark of status in England and it was no less true across the sea. Colonial gentry, like their English counterparts, imitated the aristocratic penchant for dining tables crowded with food. Conspicuous consumption was at its height.

Christmas offered unlimited opportunities for feasting. Then as now, people got together with family and friends to celebrate the holidays with the very best they had to offer. Because the Christmas season always brought a flurry of weddings, there were wedding feasts to enjoy in addition to lavish midday dinners on Christmas

OPPOSITE AND ABOVE.

A feast so bountiful that the table boards groaned under its weight was the goal of every colonial host at Christmastime. And it is still the goal at Colonial Williamsburg today, where chefs strive to create meals that follow eighteenth-century traditions. Many of their recipes are based on old "receipts" and served in surroundings reminiscent of the era. Garnishing portraits with sprigs of greenery is an ancient custom that persisted until the end of the nineteenth century.

and New Year's Day. In some Southern homes, Twelfth Night, celebrated on January 5, was the more festive occasion. "It seems," wrote one Englishman traveling through Virginia shortly before the Revolutionary War, "this is one of their annual Balls supported in the following manner: A large rich cake is provided and cut into small pieces and handed round to the company, who at the same time draws a ticket out of a Hat with something merry wrote on it. He that draws the King has the Honor of treating the company with a Ball the next year . . . . The Lady that draws the Queen has the trouble of making the Cake."

A beautifully decorated table was the focal point of every feast. There were, however, rules. Rigid visual requirements governed the proper arrangement of dishes, from the first course to

Gingerbread Cookies

(50 TO 60 COOKIES)

1 cup sugar
2 teaspoons ginger
1 teaspoon nutmeg
1 teaspoon cinnamon
$^1/_2$ teaspoon salt
1$^1/_2$ teaspoons baking soda
1 cup margarine, melted
$^1/_2$ cup evaporated milk
1 cup unsulfured molasses
$^3/_4$ teaspoon vanilla extract (optional)
$^3/_4$ teaspoon lemon extract (optional)
4 cups stone-ground or unbleached flour, unsifted

Combine the sugar, ginger, nutmeg, cinnamon, salt, and baking soda. Mix well. Add the melted margarine, evaporated milk, and molasses. Add the extracts if desired. Mix well. Add the flour 1 cup at a time, stirring constantly. The dough should be stiff enough to handle without sticking to fingers. Knead the dough for a smoother texture. Add up to $^1/_2$ cup additional flour if necessary to prevent sticking. When the dough is smooth, roll it out $^1/_4$ inch thick on a floured surface and cut it into cookies. Bake on floured or greased cookie sheets in a preheated 375° F oven for 10 to 12 minutes. The cookies are done if they spring back when touched.

OPPOSITE:
This table setting at the home of George Wythe, scholar and teacher of Thomas Jefferson, shows the elegance of gentry dining in colonial Virginia. The linen cloth has been removed for the dessert course. A rare leaded glass sweetmeat pole, laden with bits of candied fruit and sugared nuts, serves as the centerpiece. Servants or slaves would have positioned the various dishes with an eye for symmetry: Pyramids of small gingerbread cakes are precisely placed at opposite corners while tarts and other delicacies are located between.

the last. Table settings did not escape the Georgian preoccupation with symmetry: Each platter had to be balanced with a similar one on the opposite side of the table. A family's reputation rose with the number of dishes presented. Twenty or thirty per course, all precisely ordered around a centerpiece of meats or desserts, was not thought excessive.

The table was fully set and decorated before the guests sat down to dine. They would rise and leave the room after each course so that servants or slaves could clear the dishes and prepare for the next course. Throughout most of the eighteenth century, an elegant dinner consisted of two rather similar courses of meats and vegetables followed by two courses of desserts. Candlesticks graced the table only when darkness made them necessary; fresh flowers or greens were considered too "countrified" for a fashionable centerpiece. Instead, a large platter of meat or a pyramid of sweets generally occupied the middle of the table. To be sure, colonial Virginians did see flowers on the table now and then. Sugared flower petals and artificial blossoms of silk were popular, and bits of fresh flowers might be used to garnish foods, but not until the middle of the next century did large arrangements of fresh flowers become commonplace on the dinner table.

Fine white linen or damask dressed the tables during the first two courses while dessert was customarily laid on the bare wood. Serving dishes of the finest porcelain, silver, or glass were used. A pyramid of glass salvers in the center held fruits, nuts, syllabubs, sweetmeats, and other desserts; later in the century, epergnes performed the same function.

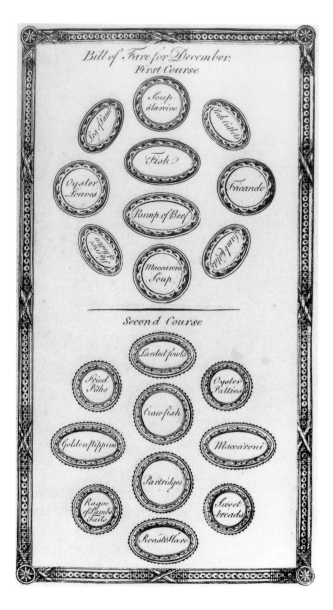

Many cookbooks of the period included sample table settings to show appropriate menus and the arrangement of
dishes. This one shows the recommended first and second
courses for a fine December dinner; the dessert course
would, by custom, have had as many dishes as the first
and second courses combined.

RIGHT:
Amid a profusion of cut glass and sterling silver, the fruit
and sweetmeat desserts in the Governor's Palace Supper
Room beckon colonial guests. By custom, the top glass of
each pyramid holds an orange.

Hostesses vied for social status through their dessert tables, presented as the grand climax to a dinner party or as a midnight entertainment during a ball. The elaborate display of sweets showcased a lady's imagination, cooking skills, artistry, and housewifely accomplishments. Appearances mattered more than taste. A good hostess concentrated on creating an eye-catching centerpiece scene—usually edible—surrounded by a profusion of symmetrically arranged desserts. The goal was a spectacle that would astonish with its originality, linger in the memories of the guests for many years, and—not incidentally—move the hostess up another rung on the social ladder.

The wealthy few employed special cooks to create miniature landscapes out of sugar, pastry, and marzipan for their holiday tables. Tiny animals molded out of colored sugar or almond paste frolicked through edible garden scenes where everything from the flowers and hedges to the swans swimming on a mirror lake was made of sugar. No doubt the head cook for Norborne Berkeley, Baron de Botetourt, Virginia's royal governor, dazzled all of Williamsburg in 1769 with his pastoral scene complete with a miniature Chinese temple—temples were quite the fad in those years—and various other dessert accessories.

Some hostesses chose to decorate with ornaments that would "serve year after year," such as figurines made of porcelain or marble (or wax, for the less affluent). Several Williamsburg shopkeepers were more than ready to oblige. Milliner Sarah Pitt advertised in the *Virginia Gazette* that she had imported from London "shapes, ornaments, and mottoes for desserts, of different sorts and figures." Guests who dined

Porcelain figures representing the continents, the four seasons, or various gods and goddesses, like this Bacchus at the Governor's Palace, graced the tables of the colonial elite. This set was made around 1765 at the Derby factory in England.

OPPOSITE:
Fresh flowers were seldom seen on fashionable tables, but edible, candied flower petals were a dessert staple.

Sugared Flower Petals

Collect edible flower petals free of insecticides (rose, violet, nasturtium, pansy, or even mint leaves); wash and gently pat dry with paper towels. Using tweezers and a clean paintbrush, coat petals with egg white then sprinkle with superfine sugar. Lay on a sheet of waxed paper to dry.

with President George Washington on Christmas Eve, 1795, remarked upon Mrs. Washington's lovely centerpiece with its plaster of Paris statuettes.

A classical mythology theme was popular at early federal dinners: Thomas Jefferson ordered four such figurines for Abigail Adams while he was in Paris. "With respect to the figures I could only find three of those you named, matched in size," he reported in a letter. "These were Minerva, Diana, and Apollo. I was obliged to add a fourth, unguided by your choice. They offered me a fine Venus," he explained gallantly, "but I thought it out of taste to have two at table at the same time." He settled on Mars.

While only the wealthiest of Virginia's gentry families could afford to entertain lavishly, modest versions of the dessert table appeared in homes of the "middling sort" as they tried to adapt the style to their own circumstances. Williamsburg ladies would have seen the most elaborate sorts of decorations when they were invited to the Governor's Palace with their husbands, as many were at Christmas in 1769 when "his Excellency the Governor gave a ball and elegant entertainment at the Palace to the Gentlemen and Ladies of this City." For their own homes, they could have purchased confectionary items such as copper molds and figurines from various local shops to create a version appropriate to their social status. Any number of cookbooks gave recipes and "Directions to set out a Table in the most elegant Manner and in the modern Taste."

"I have endeavoured to set out a desert of sweetmeats," explained Elizabeth Raffald in her 1775 book, *Experienced English Housekeeper*,

"which the industrious house-keeper may lay up at a small expense and when added to what little fruit is then in season, will make a pretty appearance after the cloth is drawn and be entertaining to the company; before you draw your cloth, have all your sweetmeats and fruits dished up in china dishes, or fruit baskets; and as many dishes as you have in one course, so many baskets or plates your dessert must have; . . . as ice is very often plentiful at that time, it will be easy to make five different ices for the middle, either to be served upon a frame or without, with four plates of dried fruit round them; apricots, green gages, grapes and pears; the four outward corners, pistachio nuts, prunelloes, oranges, and olives. The four square, nonpareils, pears, walnuts, and filberts; the two in the centre betwixt the top and bottom, chestnuts and Portugal plums; for six long dishes, pine apples, French plums, and the four brandy fruits, which are peaches, nectarines, apricots and cherries."

The traditional English Christmas dinner did not cross the Atlantic intact. The boar's heads, the roast peacocks and swans, and the Westphalia hams of merry old England were left behind; native turkeys, ducks, Virginia hams, venison, fish, and oysters took their place. Roast beef remained popular on both sides of the ocean, as did roast goose, mince pies, plum pudding, and strong drink. Lots of it.

Temperance was not a virtue. Cider, beer, and wine (homemade or imported) were commonly consumed by young and old, rich and poor, with every meal. During the Christmas season, both quality and quantity would rise. The wealthier the household, the wider the variety of beverages served, including imported

A modern-day version of the colonial style, this sideboard in the Dr. Barraud House dining room tempts guests with the bounty of the Chesapeake Bay—oysters, fish, and crabcakes. Replicas of antique porcelain, sterling silver, and glass re-create the subdued elegance of the past.

wines such as Madeira, the American favorite, or Malaga, sherry, canary, port, fayal, claret, sack, champagne, and lisbon. Stronger drink, too, was consumed: brandy, rum, gin, whiskey, and others. Even slaves had their Christmas ration of rum. A mark of hospitality was a large bowl of "punch," a generic term for a mixture of rum or brandy with sugar, fruit juice, and whatever else had been handed down through the generations in family recipe books.

Dining customs changed slowly. By the nineteenth century, the extravagances of earlier times were becoming outmoded. Many began to adopt the simpler dining style from Europe called "service à la russe." Reportedly introduced to France in 1810 by the Russian ambassador, service à la russe banished nearly everything from the dinner table except the individual place settings and a centerpiece. As guests admired the fresh flowers and candelabra in the middle of the table, servants brought in one or two dishes at a time and served each person individually. Although many in the United States clung fast to the old dining customs until well into the nineteenth century, service à la russe ultimately prevailed. At the same time, the introduction of the Christmas tree pulled the decorating emphasis away from the dining room and into the parlor.

OPPOSITE:
Punch is served in the home of Thomas Everard. The word "punch" probably derives from the Hindustani word for "five," the number of ingredients found in this popular beverage: water, sugar, citrus juice, spices, and, of course, some form of wine or spirits. The recipe and proportions were left to individual tastes. If the two most expensive ingredients, citrus and spices, were left out, a poor man's "toddy" or "bumbo" resulted.

A Fine Punch

Pour the strained Juice of two large Oranges over three-fourths of a Pound of Loaf-Sugar. Add a little of the outside Peel cut in very thin Slices. Pour over it one Quart of boiling Water, one Pint of Arrack [substitute rum], and a Pint of hot red French Wine. Stir together. This may be served when cold and will improve with Age.

Shield's Tavern Syllabubs

(6 TO 8 SERVINGS)

1½ cups whipping cream
Rind and juice of 2 lemons
½ cup sugar
½ cup white wine
¼ cup dry sherry
Whipped cream (optional)

Whisk the whipping cream by hand until it thickens a bit. Add the lemon rind, lemon juice, sugar, wine, and sherry, one at a time, whisking by hand after each addition. Whisk the mixture for 3 to 5 minutes until thickened. Keep in mind that too much whipping will turn it to butter. Pour it immediately into parfait glasses and refrigerate overnight. The mixture will separate when it stands. If desired, pile whipped cream on top of each glass before serving.

OPPOSITE:
In the spirit of the eighteenth century, Williamsburg chefs whip up modern versions of trifles, syllabubs, and fruit tarts, adapting old recipes to today's palate.

Colonial Williamsburg Christmas Tables

"In the middle of the table was placed a piece of table furniture about six feet long and two feet wide, rounded at the ends. It was either of wood gilded, or polished metal, raised about an inch with a silver rim round it like that round a tea board; in the centre was a pedestal of plaster of Paris with images upon it, and on each end figures; male and female, of the same. It was very elegant and used for ornament only. The dishes were placed all around, and there was an elegant variety of roast beef, veal, turkeys, ducks, fowls, hams, etc. puddings, jellies, oranges, apples, nuts, almonds, figs, raisins, and a variety of wines and punch."

—A dinner with President and Mrs. George Washington,
Christmas Eve 1795

During the 1930s and 1940s when Colonial Williamsburg's Christmas traditions were starting to coalesce, dining tables throughout the Historic Area were decorated in a manner thought to be reminiscent of the eighteenth century. Bowls of fruit punctuated with pine or holly sprigs and sterling silver epergnes laden with fruit and nuts took center stage with an occasional assist from a cornucopia spilling its contents onto the table. Today, this decorating style is known as Colonial Revival. It was not an accurate re-creation of the eighteenth-century style nor was it meant to be, but the Colonial Revival movement achieved widespread popularity by translating the earlier era into a visual language twentieth-century Americans could readily appreciate.

Once again, Mrs. Fisher's inspiration had come from della Robbia garlands and Grinling Gibbons carvings. She also used Robert Furber's fruit and flower prints to show what varieties were appropriate to the colonial period. Ever mindful of the eighteenth-century requirement for symmetry, she laid satin ribbons diagonally across dining tables and placed pieces of fruit on them; she assembled great apple pyramids crowned with large pineapples and encircled punch bowls with wreaths.

Although not strictly accurate to the eighteenth century, Mrs. Fisher's tables were widely admired and widely imitated. Women's magazines, craft books, and Christmas decorating guides featured the new old-fashioned decorations and showed how they could be assembled at home with materials available locally. At a time when the country looked to the past for stylistic inspiration, the Williamsburg decorations caught the imagination of people who wanted to recapture the gracious life-style of a bygone era without actually reproducing it.

During the 1980s, a new commitment to authenticity led Colonial Williamsburg to turn the corner with its Christmas decorating. Based on solid new historical research on eighteenth-century dining customs, the effort to replicate the recipes, techniques, and ingredients of the time assured that holiday tables could at long last be portrayed in all their glory—the way they would have looked moments before the guests walked into the room.

English and continental cookbooks and print sources provided clues about how tables were set and decorated; Virginia diaries and other personal accounts lent local detail. Food specialists developed a way to make natural-looking fake foods, thus freeing the curators from worries about spoilage. Thanks to a cooperative effort between food preparers, historians, and curatorial staff, what visitors saw happening in the restored kitchens coordinated with what was on the table in the dining rooms. Christmas interiors had become more accurate and more lavish all at once.

While Virginia colonists did not consider flower arrangements appropriate for dining tables, dried flowers and winter greenery did appear on other tables and mantels in bedchambers and parlors during the winter months. Holly with its crimson berries was a Christmas favorite that is pictured in English prints of the period.

OPPOSITE:
Guests were always welcome in colonial Virginia but never more so than during the Christmas season when they provided an agreeable diversion during the long winter evenings. In larger gentry homes, a spare bedroom might be occupied for weeks on end as extended family, friends, and travelers came to visit.

Fruit Pyramids

"[There were] many little iced cakes and rosy apples in pyramids."

—Constance Cary Harrison, on a Virginia dinner
during the Civil War

Arranged on a bed of boxwood and lady apples, these miniature pineapples are similar to those available to Virginians during the colonial period. This delectable New World fruit soon became a royal favorite in England and something of a fashion statement on wealthy dining tables.

The single most enduring Williamsburg table decoration—and still the most popular—is the fruit pyramid. Appearing in European prints as early as the seventeenth century and on Virginia dinner tables from the colonial period through the Civil War, the pyramid was one of the first table decorations used when Colonial Williamsburg began to decorate for Christmas. Originally a careful stacking of fruits, small cookies, or candied sweetmeats that was meant to be consumed at the end of the meal, the pyramid has evolved into something purely decorative—and less apt to tumble off the table, thanks to the modern invention of the wooden apple cone.

When Colonial Williamsburg's carpenters first pounded some headless nails into a chunk of wood, no one had any idea that the simple device would be met with such public enthusiasm. So many visitors asked for the "secret" to the apple pyramid that Colonial Williamsburg started handing out instructions on how to make the wooden forms at home. The versatile fruit pyramid—never quite extinct in Virginia—was back in the national limelight.

There are as many ways to make a fruit pyramid as there are fruits, but bright red or green apples remain the favorite for Christmas tables. Traditionally, fruit or sweetmeat pyramids were topped with sprigs of holly or with another piece of fruit. At Colonial Williamsburg the pineapple became the favorite crown.

While it would certainly have been a hospitable gesture for a host to serve his guests such a treat, there is no documentation for the oft-repeated adage that the pineapple symbolized hospitality in colonial America. In recent years, the Colonial Williamsburg staff has begun using smaller varieties of fruits in the Historic Area in recognition of the fact that today's hybrids are significantly larger than their eighteenth-century counterparts. One of these is a miniature pineapple grown in the West Indies that closely resembles the pineapples available to Virginia colonists—the wealthy colonists, that is. These are used on fruit pyramids and apple fans and are affixed to wreaths throughout the Historic Area.

Though purely decorative today, fruit pyramids were an edible fixture on European and colonial dessert tables at least as early as the seventeenth century. Initially these pyramids were made with sweetmeats, berries, or some small fruit such as cherries or grapes, packed with sugar in a cone-shaped tin mold, and removed to stand on a platter until consumed by the guests. Larger fruits were carefully stacked. The development in the twentieth century of the conical-shaped wooden form studded with nails gave new life to the decorative fruit pyramid.

Candles

"Instead of being disagreeable, if an Accident puts a [bayberry] Candle out, it yields a pleasant Fragrancy to all that are in the Room; insomuch that nice People often put them out, on purpose to have the Incense of their expiring Snuff."

—*Robert Beverley, 1705*

Perhaps it was inevitable that bayberry candles should come to be associated with a Virginia Christmas. Bayberries (also known as wax myrtle berries or candleberries) grow wild along much of the East Coast, and they mature in November and December. The natural green color of the wax and its delicate fragrance add to the Christmas imagery.

There were several choices for candles in preelectric America. Those who could afford the best purchased spermaceti candles made from the waxy substance from the head of a sperm whale; those who could not dipped their own tallow candles from animal fat or, if they were more for-tunate, beeswax. None of these candles had the fresh scent or long-lasting qualities of the bayberry.

Using bayberries for candlemaking was new to the English colonists. Robert Beverley, an early Virginia planter, wrote of the "very modern" discovery in 1705: "At the Mouth of their Rivers, and all along upon the Sea and Bay, and near many of their Creeks and Swamps, grows the Myrtle, bearing a Berry, of which they make a hard brittle Wax, of a curious green Colour, which by refining becomes almost transparent. Of this they make Candles, which are never greasie to the Touch, nor melt with lying in the hottest Weather: Neither does the Snuff of these ever offend the Smell, like that of a Tallow-Candle."

Regardless of his fascination for bayberry candles, Beverley did not use them—or any sort of candle—on his dining room table unless the meal was being served after dark. Not until Victorian times did the candle take on its purely decorative daylight role.

Genuine bayberry wax and ready-made bayberry candles are hard to come by today, but their spicy fragrance is pure Christmas.

OPPOSITE:
Tedious to make and expensive to buy, the bayberry candle was a rarity in colonial America. The bush grows abundantly in coastal regions from Nova Scotia to North Carolina yet its berries are so small that thousands are required to make even a single candle. The berries are boiled in water until their waxy coating floats on the top. The bayberry wax, a dusky green color, is skimmed off and poured into a candle mold to harden.

CHAPTER FIVE

A Colonial Revival Christmas

"Now Christmas comes, 'tis fit that we
Should feast and sing, and merry be
Keep open House, let Fiddlers play
A fig for cold, sing Care away."

—The Virginia Almanack, *1766*

In the huge entrance hall of Carter's Grove, the 1755 brick plantation house located just outside Williamsburg on the banks of the James River, stands an enormous Christmas tree covered with twentieth-century ornaments. Within the Historic Area at Bassett Hall, the eighteenth-century frame house once used as the Rockefellers' Williamsburg residence, a small Christmas tree sits on a table. Carnations, poinsettias, and other nineteenth-century flowers and ribbons decorate the house. Gaily colored Christmas tree balls are piled in a bowl on the table. Clearly none of this is correct for the colonial period.

Both houses are decorated in the early-

OPPOSITE AND ABOVE:
In colonial days, plantation houses such as Carter's Grove faced the water because the river was the highway that brought both people and supplies. The shell theme in the front entrance decoration reminds today's visitors of the river's importance to plantation life.

twentieth-century Colonial Revival style, from the furnishings down to the Christmas finery. The Colonial Revival is that quintessentially American style of interior design that began in 1876 with the centennial of the nation's birth. Patriotism and nostalgia for the "good old days" guided proponents of the Colonial Revival toward an increased appreciation of early American architecture, antiques, history, heroes, and genealogy. The restoration of Williamsburg (indeed, the restoration of a great many historic homes and villages that followed close on the heels of the Rockefellers' massive undertaking) is as much a product of the Colonial Revival as it is the cause of the revival's continued strength throughout the twentieth century.

93

First settled by the English in 1620, the land on the banks of the wide James River was purchased by Robert ("King") Carter early in the eighteenth century for his daughter Elizabeth. In his will, he requested that the property be called Carter's Grove, and through various owners and tenants, the name has persisted. The original house, completed in 1755, was substantially altered in the 1930s, making it more Colonial Revival in style than colonial. Every Christmas, the house is decorated inside and out in a Colonial Revival manner.

No attempt was made in Colonial Revival interiors to replicate the true colonial appearance. Rather, it was a more romanticized version of that era, a glorification of its virtues and quaint charms that shrewdly retained the essentials of modern comfort such as overstuffed chairs, thick Oriental rugs, and electric lamps. In recent years, architects and historians have come to view the Colonial Revival as a distinct style worthy of study and preservation on its own merits. For that reason, Colonial Williams-

burg made the decision to restore Carter's Grove plantation and Bassett Hall to the Colonial Revival period (the 1930s and 1940s) rather than take the houses back to their earlier eighteenth-century origins.

In many ways, the Williamsburg Christmas is a Colonial Revival Christmas, a holiday that captures the essence of our nation's colonial heritage by using the materials and customs of that era and adapting them to the modern meaning of Christmas.

In the grand entrance hall at Carter's Grove, the ribbon entwined through the pine roping, the red and white floral arrangements, the large boxwood kissing ball, and the ceiling-to-floor Christmas tree are twentieth-century interpretations of eighteenth- and nineteenth-century practices.

Lady apples orbit a large Osage orange like planets around a sun. Aucuba, variegated holly, and bayberry lend texture and color to the greenery in this Bassett Hall entrance decoration.

LEFT:
Set back among the trees at the end of a shady approach is Bassett Hall, the Williamsburg home of Mr. and Mrs. John D. Rockefeller, Jr. The family stayed here whenever they came to Williamsburg until 1979, when Bassett Hall and its 585 woodland acres were given to Colonial Williamsburg. The decorating staff finds some of its Christmas greenery in this pristine forest.

Mrs. Rockefeller furnished Bassett Hall with a comfortable mixture of old and new. Massed in the morning room fireplace are creamy pink poinsettias. Poinsettias were brought to the attention of Americans by diplomat Joel Roberts Poinsett, the country's first ambassador to the newly formed Mexican republic in 1825. An amateur botanist, Poinsett sent specimens of the native plant back to the States, where it became the principal flower of the Christmas season.

OPPOSITE:
In the dining room at Bassett Hall, wrapped presents cluster beneath a tabletop tree decorated with twentieth-century orna-ments. While the custom of exchanging Christmas gifts is thought to have originated in the nineteenth century, a 1577 poem suggests it could have been a revival of a much older practice: "At Christmas of Christ many Carols we sing / And give many gifts in the joy of that King."

Into the Twenty-First Century

"I have shared with you the light from my Christmas Eve candle. I have set it in the window of my soul which faces the house where you dwell."

—W. A. R. Goodwin, December 24, 1935

Not everyone lives in an eighteenth-century house or wants to decorate as if he or she does. In spite of that, the Williamsburg Christmas style has moved comfortably across the country and into homes that have little in common with their symmetrical Georgian predecessors.

Adaptable and versatile, the Williamsburg Christmas travels well, requiring no set list of ingredients, no particular climate or religious belief. If nature cannot supply magnolia leaves and cotton bolls, it borrows rhododendron or pinecones. If Osage oranges and chinaberries are unavailable, green apples and yarrow satisfy just as well and add a dash of local color besides. Americans have been inviting the traditional Williamsburg Christmas into their homes for more than half a century. In the best Colonial Revival tradition, they translate the designs, objects, or customs of the eighteenth century into modern vernacular and, in doing so, enrich the visual vocabulary of our country's premier holiday.

Homeowners can interpret a Colonial Williamsburg Christmas into a distinctly noncolonial celebration, according to the architectural style and furnishings of their own homes. Ideas include a rambling Tudor Revival house with an Arts and Crafts interior, built at the dawn of the twentieth century where the city once met the country; a 1906 urban town

Instead of the festoons of fresh evergreens that we associate with a historical Christmas, a ribbon tumbles down the rail of this Arts and Crafts–style staircase, visually linking a dozen dried cockscomb wreaths. The red wreaths were sized to match the circular design element in the woodwork behind them.

OPPOSITE:

The Arts and Crafts movement influenced the interior design of this Tudor Revival home, recently restored to its original appearance. Colonial-era ingredients arranged in a more naturalistic manner give the 1908 house its own version of Christmas style. An asymmetrical garland made of grapevine interwoven with dried pomegranate, cockscomb, sumac berries, poet's laurel, and cedar frames the front door view.

ABOVE AND OPPOSITE:
A fresh fruit ring around the punch bowl revives the della Robbia style in the early-twentieth-century dining room. A modern version of the colonial dessert course has been spread on the bare table. On the mantel, twin topiaries of boxwood are dressed with clusters of nandina berries instead of the traditional holly.

This compact town house reflects the eclectic taste of its bachelor owner. The gilded symmetry of the dining room carries over to its Christmas decoration: Gilded lotus pods, holly leaves, and pinecones are arranged on the mantel; on the table, miniature apple cones on a bed of gilded magnolia leaves flank an antique Chinese Foo dog.

OPPOSITE:

The staircase receives special treatment with plain pine roping and a newel-post plaque made with dried artichoke, lotus pods, wheat, sensitive fern, okra pods, and one red apple. A unique wrought-iron Christmas tree is ornamented with lady apples.

house, the layout of which is similar to many American homes; and a spacious Southwest-style home filled with sunlight and antiques collected by a couple who left their hearts in Santa Fe. In every small town, in every bustling city, in every state in America there are houses and apartments where the Williamsburg Christmas may be adapted to contemporary lifestyles.

ABOVE AND OPPOSITE:

The exuberance and colors of the Southwest rule this contemporary home. Abundance is the law: on the front door, the inviting wreath of pomegranates, kumquats, red peppers, apples, tangerines, and clementines sets the stage for the main event inside. The symmetrical placement of fruit and ribbons so prominent on Colonial Revival dining tables takes a Southwest accent with its bold colors. Ostrich eggs give the traditional fruit centerpiece an untraditional twist.

Traditional mixes effortlessly with contemporary in the breakfast room. The turquoise of the walls highlights the fresh lemons in the pyramid and on the wreaths, and tiny lemon rind baskets full of holly berries accent each place setting.

San Ysidro, patron saint of farmers, surveys the holiday harvest. His outstretched hand offers a bunch of red peppers; more are fastened, with lady apples, in the swag at his feet. The wooden saint and the chair below him date from Mexico's colonial period.

At a time when shrill commercialism threatens to smother the old-fashioned holidays, the Colonial Williamsburg Christmas focuses on home, family, and hospitality, values that Americans share. The holiday means the fragrance of fresh-cut pine roping clinging to the banister, the candles winking like starlight through cloudy windowpanes, the crackle of a hot fire on a cold night, and the bounty of winter fruits and greens that decorate the dining room table. For a Williamsburg Christmas, the spotlight is on tradition, the stars are the children who string the popcorn and cranberries, the mothers who bake the gingerbread men, and the fathers who haul out the ladder and hoist the apple fan over the front door.

Christmas has evolved profoundly over past centuries, and Colonial Williamsburg played an important role in defining the way we celebrate what has become a cherished holiday. Along the way, the Williamsburg style sparked a renewed appreciation for homemade decorations and a respect for natural materials. But a Williamsburg Christmas decorates the house with more than fruits and greenery—it hangs up pride in America's heritage, shines welcome from the windows, and sets hospitality on the table. And like a good guest, it leaves the house a little warmer for the visit.

"We wish you health, and good fires; victuals, drink, and good stomachs; innocent diversion, and good company; honest trading, and good success; loving courtship, and good wives; and lastly, a merry CHRISTMAS and a happy NEW YEAR."

—The Virginia Almanack, *1771*

Complete references to books and articles cited are found in the bibliography.

CHAPTER ONE: CHRISTMAS IN COLONIAL TIMES

Page 19:
"I hope you have spent . . . for a Christmas Box." Letter from Henry Tucker to his brother St. George Tucker, January 4, 1773, in Mary Goodwin, *Christmas in Colonial Virginia.*

Page 20:
"After Breakfast . . . too dark to dance." Hunter Dickinson Farish, ed., *The Journal and Letters of Philip Vickers Fithian,* pp. 33–34.

Page 23:
"It was near twelve . . . fruits, etc." Jane Carson, *Colonial Virginians at Play,* p. 9.

Page 27:
"Nothing is now to be heard . . . at the approaching Christmas." Hunter Dickinson Farish, ed., *The Journal and Letters of Philip Vickers Fithian,* p. 34.
   "Whosoever shall be found . . . five shillings." James A. Cox, "Saving Christmas in the Colonies," p. 15.
   "The Feast of Christ's Nativity . . . by Rude Reveling." Stephen Nissenbaum, *The Battle for Christmas,* p. 7.

Page 28:
"Against the Feast of Christmas . . . likewise, garnished." Alexander Tille, *Yule and Christmas, Their Place in the Germanic Year,* pp. 105–106.
   "Pews and altar . . . are green in winter time." David DeSimone, "Another Look at Christmas in the Eighteenth Century," p. 6.

Page 31:
"From every hedge . . . verdant garb confess." Nathan B. Warren, *The Christmas Book: Christmas in the Olden Time,* p. 13.
   "Get Iuye and hull, woman, deck vp thyne house." Thomas Tusser, *Five Hundred Pointes of Good Husbandrie,* p. 225.

Page 32:
"I was waked . . . all round the House." Hunter Dickinson Farish, ed., *The Journal and Letters of Philip Vickers Fithian,* p. 39.
   "All over the Colony . . . to be invited." Colonial Williamsburg research file, "Christmas," *London Magazine,* 1746.

CHAPTER TWO: WILLIAMSBURG CHRISTMAS TRADITIONS

Page 35:
"The damsel donn'd . . . gather in the mistletoe." Sir Walter Scott, "Marmion," *Scott: Poetical Works,* p. 152.

Page 37:
"He said his holiday . . . ninety-five of 'em!" Colonial Williamsburg's *Christmas Decoration Training Manual,* 1992, unpublished, p. 9.

Page 38:
"These dear Virginians! . . . with these Virginians." Newspaper article, n.d., in Valentine Museum, Richmond, VA, "Christmas Virginia."
   "Went to Pohick church and returned to dinner." Mary Goodwin, *Christmas in Colonial Virginia,* p. xvii.

Page 40:
"With holly and ivy . . . fresh as the day." Nathan B. Warren, *The Christmas Book: Christmas in the Olden Time,* p. 31.

Page 42:
"The Palace or Governor's House . . . occasional rejoicings." Hugh Jones, *The Present State of Virginia,* p. 70.
   "were set with a double row of candles." *The Journal of Francis Louis Michel,* p. 128.

Page 48:
"The College of William and Mary . . . better than white ones." Memo from John Stewart Bryan, President, College of William and Mary, December 10, 1940, Colonial Williamsburg Archives.

Page 51:
"When it was to begin . . . set off the fireworks." *The Journal of Francis Louis Michel*, p. 128.

"A firemaster was considered the most expert . . . and praised them highly." *The Journal of Francis Louis Michel*, p. 128.

Page 52:
"The days before Christmas . . . sprigs of holly." Memoirs of Nancy Keene Perkins Lancaster, n.d., p. 3, Virginia Historical Society, Richmond, Va.

CHAPTER THREE: DECK THE DOORS

Page 57:
"The Rooms were embower'd . . . Country Milkmaid." *Round about Our Coal-Fire*, p. 1.

"Of late years . . . terra cottas of the Renaissance." Elizabeth Russell, "Wreaths and Swags," p. 695.

CHAPTER FOUR: GROANING BOARDS

Page 73:
"At Christmas be mery . . . the great and the small." Thomas Tusser, *Five Hundred Pointes of Good Husbandrie*, p. 225.

"It seems . . . the trouble of making the Cake." *The Journal of Nicholas Cresswell*, pp. 52–53.

Page 74:
Gingerbread cookie recipe from Mary Miley Theobald, *Recipes from the Raleigh Tavern Bake Shop*, p. 5.

Page 76:
Table setting diagram from John Farley, *London Art of Cookery, and Housekeeper's Complete Assistant*, plate [12].

Page 79:
"serve year after year." Hannah Glasse, *The Compleat Confectioner*, p. 255.

"shapes, ornaments . . . different sorts and figures." *Virginia Gazette* (Purdie & Dixon), December 14, 1769.

Page 80:
"With respect to the figures . . . at the same time." *Writings of Thomas Jefferson*, p. 99.

"His Excellency . . . and Ladies of the City." *Virginia Gazette* (Purdie & Dixon), December 28, 1769.

"Directions to set out a Table . . . peaches, nectarines, apricots and cherries." Elizabeth Raffald, *Experienced English Housekeeper*, p. 382.

Page 83:
Punch recipe from Helen Bullock, *The Williamsburg Art of Cookery*, p. 217.

Page 84:
Syllabub recipe from the *Williamsburg Cookbook*, p. 125.

"In the middle of the table . . . wines and punch." Letter from Theophilus Bradbury, December 26, 1795, in Mary Goodwin, *Christmas in Colonial Virginia*, p. xxxix.

Page 88:
"[There were] many little iced cakes and rosy apples in pyramids." Constance Cary Harrison, *Recollections Grave and Gay*, p. 170.

Page 90:
"Instead of being disagreeable . . . expiring Snuff." Robert Beverley, *The History and Present State of Virginia in Four Parts*, pp. 137–138.

"At the Mouth of their Rivers . . . of a Tallow-Candle." Robert Beverley, *The History and Present State of Virginia in Four Parts*, pp. 137–138.

CHAPTER FIVE: A COLONIAL REVIVAL CHRISTMAS

Page 93:
"Now Christmas comes . . . sing Care away." *Virginia Almanack*, 1766, in Mary Goodwin, *Christmas in Colonial Virginia*, p. 16.

Page 99:
"At Christmas of Christ . . . the joy of that King." Thomas Tusser, *Five Hundred Pointes of Good Husbandrie*, p. 68.

Page 100:
"I have shared . . . the house where you dwell." Dennis Montgomery, *A Link Among the Days*, p. 275.

Page 110:
"We wish you health . . . and a happy NEW YEAR." *The Virginia Almanack for the Year of our Lord God 1771* in Mary Goodwin, *Christmas in Colonial Virginia*, p. xviii.

Diagrams on pages 120–125 for wreaths, apple cones, and apple fans are taken from Libbey Hodges Oliver, *Colonial Williamsburg Decorates for Christmas*, pp. 20–21, 42–43, 34–36.

Children's toys were advertised for sale by Williamsburg merchants and milliners, but the association of toys with Christmas was not established until later, during the nineteenth century. Some children did receive a "Christmas box" gift of a few coins or even a book, but toys came at other occasions.

Bibliography

Barnett, James H. *American Christmas: A Study in National Culture.* New York: Macmillan Co., 1954.

Belden, Louise C. "The Colonial Dessert Table," *Antiques,* December 1975.

———. *The Festive Tradition: Table Decoration and Desserts in America, 1650–1900.* New York: W. W. Norton & Co., 1983.

Beverley, Robert. *The History and Present State of Virginia in Four Parts* (originally published in London: R. Parker, 1705). Edited by Louis B. Wright. Chapel Hill, NC: University of North Carolina Press, 1947.

Booth, Letha, and Joan Parry Dutton. *The Williamsburg Cookbook.* 10th ed. Williamsburg, VA: Colonial Williamsburg, 1992.

Bullock, Helen. *The Williamsburg Art of Cookery.* Williamsburg, VA: 1938.

Carson, Jane. *Colonial Virginians at Play.* Williamsburg, VA: Colonial Williamsburg, 1989.

Cassell's Household Guide: A Complete Encyclopaedia of Domestic and Social Economy. Vol. I. London: Cassell, Petter, & Galpin, 1875.

Chambers, W. *Book of Days.* Vol. II: "December." London: W. & R. Chambers, 1862–64.

Chinard, Gilbert, ed. *A Huguenot Exile in Virginia.* New York: Press of the Pioneers, 1934. The Journal of Durand of Dauphiné, 1687.

Colonial Williamsburg Research File, "Christmas." *London Magazine,* 1746.

Cox, James A. "Saving Christmas in the Colonies," *Colonial Williamsburg Journal,* Winter 1990–91.

Cresswell, Nicholas. *The Journal of Nicholas Cresswell.* New York: Dial Press, 1928.

Davis, Hubert J. *Christmas in the Mountains.* Murfreesboro, NC: Johnson Publishing Co., 1972.

DelRe, Gerard, and Patricia DelRe. *Christmas Almanack.* New York: Doubleday & Co., 1979.

Dennison's Christmas Book: Decorations and Novelties for Use in Homes, Halls, Clubs, Schoolrooms and Churches. Boston: Dennison Manufacturing Co., 1921.

DeSimone, David. "Another Look at Christmas in the Eighteenth Century." *Colonial Williamsburg Interpreter,* Winter 1995–96.

———. "The Christmas Box Tradition," *Colonial Williamsburg Interpreter,* Winter 1996–97.

Farish, Hunter Dickinson, ed. *The Journal and Letters of Philip Vickers Fithian.* Williamsburg, VA: Colonial Williamsburg, 1957.

Farley, John. *London Art of Cookery, and Housekeeper's Complete Assistant.* London: 1796.

Fisher, Louise. *An Eighteenth-Century Garland.* Williamsburg, VA: Colonial Williamsburg, 1951.

———. "Evergreen Decking at Christmas," Colonial Williamsburg Research Report, 1939.

Foley, Daniel J. *The Christmas Tree.* Philadelphia: Chilton Co., 1960.

Glasse, Hannah. *The Compleat Confectioner.* London: 1770.

Goodwin, Mary R. M. *Christmas in Colonial Virginia.* Williamsburg, VA: Colonial Williamsburg, 1955.

————. *The Colonial Store.* Williamsburg, VA: Colonial Williamsburg, 1966.

Harrison, Constance Cary. *Recollections Grave and Gay.* New York: Charles Scribner's Sons, 1911.

Hottes, Alfred C. *1001 Christmas Facts and Fancies.* New York: Dodd, Mead & Co., 1937.

Howell, Wendy. "Setting a Fine Table: The Christmas Season." *Colonial Williamsburg Interpreter,* Winter 1996–97.

Jefferson, Thomas. *Writings of Thomas Jefferson.* Edited by Paul Leicester Ford. New York: G. P. Putnam's Sons, 1894.

Jones, Hugh. *The Present State of Virginia* (originally published in London, 1724). Edited by Richard L. Morton. Chapel Hill, NC: University of North Carolina Press, 1956.

Kane, Harnett T. *The Southern Christmas Book.* New York: D. McKay Co., 1958.

Lamond, Marguerite Moncure. "How to Make a Wreath in the Della Robbia Style," *Flower and Garden,* December 1976.

Lewis, Taylor Biggs, Jr., and Joanne B. Young. *Christmas in Williamsburg.* Williamsburg, VA: Colonial Williamsburg, 1970.

Miall, Antony, and Peter Miall. *The Victorian Christmas Book.* New York: Pantheon Books, 1978.

Michel, Francis Louis. "The Journal of Francis Louis Michel," 1702. Translated and edited by William J. Hinke. *The Virginia Magazine of History and Biography,* April 1916.

Miles, Clement A. *Christmas in Ritual and Tradition, Christian and Pagan.* London: T. Fisher Unwin, 1912.

Montgomery, Dennis. *A Link Among the Days: The Life and Times of the Reverend Doctor W. A. R. Goodwin, the Father of Colonial Williamsburg.* Richmond, VA: Dietz Press, 1998.

Nissenbaum, Stephen. *The Battle for Christmas.* New York: Alfred A. Knopf, 1996.

Noël Hume, Ivor. "'Twas the Day After Christmas . . . ," *Colonial Williamsburg Journal,* Autumn 1997.

Oliver, Libbey. *Colonial Williamsburg Decorates for Christmas.* Williamsburg, VA: Colonial Williamsburg, 1981.

Oliver, Libbey, and Mary Theobald. "Deck the Doors," *Colonial Williamsburg Journal,* Winter 1996–97.

————. "Deck the Halls," *Colonial Williamsburg Journal,* Autumn 1997.

————. "Lighting the Town," *Colonial Williamsburg Journal,* Autumn 1995.

Olmert, Michael. "The Hospitable Pineapple," *Colonial Williamsburg Journal,* Winter 1997–98.

Powers, Emma L. "Christmas Customs," *Colonial Williamsburg Interpreter,* Winter 1995–96.

Raffald, Elizabeth. *Experienced English Housekeeper.* London: 1775.

Recipes from the Raleigh Tavern Bake Shop. Williamsburg, VA: Colonial Williamsburg, 1984.

Restad, Penne L. *Christmas in America: A History.* New York: Oxford University Press, 1995.

Round about Our Coal-Fire; or, Christmas Entertainments. London: F. Roberts, ca. 1740.

Rountree, Susan Hight. *Christmas Decorations from Williamsburg.* Williamsburg, VA: Colonial Williamsburg, 1991.

Rulon, Philip R. *Keeping Christmas.* Hamden, CT: Archon Books, 1990.

Russell, Elizabeth H. "Wreaths and Swags," *House Beautiful Magazine*, December 1926.

Scott, Walter, Sir. "Marmion." Edited by J. Logie Robertson. *Scott: Poetical Works.* London: Oxford University Press, 1904.

Sheppard, Donna C. *A Williamsburg Christmas.* Williamsburg, VA: Colonial Williamsburg, 1980.

Smith, Eliza. *The Compleat Housewife.* London: 1758. Facsimile of 16th edition, Herts. England: Arlon House Publishing, 1983.

Theobald, Mary. "Illuminating the Grand Illumination," *William and Mary Alumni Gazette,* December 1997.

Tille, Alexander. *Yule and Christmas, Their Place in the Germanic Year.* London: David Nutt, 1899.

Tusser, Thomas. *Five Hundred Pointes of Good Husbandrie* (1580 edition collated with those of 1573 and 1577). Edited by W. Payne & Sidney J. Herrtage. London: Trubner and Co., 1878. (Vaduz: Kraus Reprint 1965).

Warren, Nathan B. *The Christmas Book: Christmas in the Olden Time.* London: J. Pattie, 1859.

TOP RIGHT AND RIGHT:

The Hartwell Perry Ordinary served meals and beverages and rented beds to travelers during the years after the Revolutionary War. The tavern's sign is done in rebus form, with pictures standing for the words. Above the trees is a hart, the Middle English word for a male deer; below him is a well. In the trees are pears which were used to make a popular fermented drink called perry. Pears are not often used on Williamsburg door decorations because they spoil so quickly, but at the Hartwell Perry Ordinary, the connection is too strong to ignore.

Products List

Many of the products shown on these pages are available for sale. For information on these items and other products sold through the Colonial Williamsburg Foundation, please call Retail Customer Service, 1-800-770-5938.

Page 4 Cresset; Page 6 Bird Bottle, Playing Cards; Page 8 Governor's Palace Candlestick; Page 9 Teardrop Stemware; Page 19 Dotware Bank; Page 21 Octagonal Base Candlesticks; Page 25 Hurricane Shades, Teardrop Stemware, Stoneware Mug and Pitcher; Page 29 Bruton Hurricane Sconces; Page 37 Fireplace Andirons; Page 49 Cresset; Page 54 Furber Flower Prints; Page 55 Furber Fruit Prints; Page 57 Clay Pipes; Page 69 Fan Plaque for Decorating; Page 70 Bird Bottle, Clay Pipes; Page 71 Playing Cards; Page 72 Duke of Gloucester Dinnerware, Airtwist Stemware; Page 75 Airtwist Stemware; Page 82 Teardrop Stemware, Hurricane Shade; Page 85 Octagonal Base Candlestick, Fireplace Andirons, Shrub Glasses, Fireplace Fender; Page 86 Swirl Base Candlestick; Page 89 Apple Cone Form; Page 91 Swirl Base Candlestick, Octagonal Base Candlestick, Straw Hat, Bayberry Candles; Page 95 Carter's Stone Lamp; Page 104 Apple Cone Form; Page 108 Apple Cone Form

Other products available from the Colonial Williamsburg Foundation:

BOOKS

Colonial Williamsburg Decorates for Christmas: Step-by-Step Illustrated Instructions for Christmas Decorations That You Can Make for Your Home, by Libbey Hodges Oliver, softbound, 80 pages. How-to directions for making 42 Williamsburg-style decorations—wreaths, apple and lemon cones, kissing balls, and accents for banisters and sconces.

Entertaining Ideas from Williamsburg, by Susan Hight Rountree, hardbound, 160 pages.
Offers a wealth of flower-arranging, decorating, handicraft, and cooking ideas for celebrating Christmas.

Christmas Decorations from Williamsburg, by Susan Hight Rountree, hardbound, 144 pages. Ideas and instructions to create seasonal wreaths, swags, roping, and decorations for mantels, stairways, windows, and tables. Fresh and dried plant materials used in both traditional and contemporary ways are featured.

VIDEO

Christmas Decorations from Williamsburg, VHS videocassette, running time 70 minutes.
Step-by-step demonstrations show how to shape flowers, fresh fruits, greens, berries, dried pods, and cones into traditional and contemporary holiday pieces.

List of Plant Materials

Winter Plant Materials Generally
Available to Colonial Virginians

apples, red and green
lady apples
lemons
limes
oranges
miniature pineapples
pomegranates
cranberries
holly berries
bayberries
chinaberries
rose hips
beauty berries
sumac berries
bittersweet berries
magnolia pods
dried flowers: globe amaranth, strawflowers,
    yarrow, cockscomb
milkweed pods
lotus pods
honesty (money plant)
cotton bolls
okra pods
Japanese lantern
dried cayenne peppers
holm (live oak)
holly
rosemary
laurel
ivy
mistletoe
magnolia

red cedar
red oak
yew
boxwood
ground pine
pine
leucothoe
fir
anise tree
mountain laurel

Plant Materials Not Generally
Available to Virginians until the
Nineteenth Century

kumquats
pepper berries
popcorn tree
Osage orange
nandina berries
pyracantha berries
heather
poinsettias
peanuts

Please help conserve native plants by avoiding the use of rare or endangered species, especially ground pine, running cedar, running pine, and mountain laurel.

Mixed Fruit Wreath

> *1 18-inch basic boxwood or evergreen wreath
> on a frame*
> *32 pieces of #16-gauge floral wire in 18-inch
> lengths*
> *4 small pomegranates*
> *Wire cutters*
> *12 lady apples that are uniform in size*
> *12 lemons that are uniform in size*
> *4 small oranges*
> *6 4-inch floral picks*
> *6 magnolia pods that are uniform in size*
> *4- to 6-inch sprigs of pyracantha with berries*

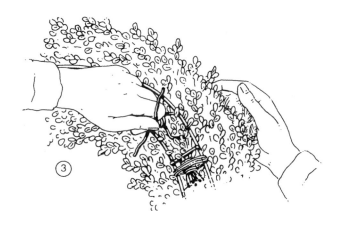

Push a piece of wire midway through the side center of each pomegranate, lady apple, lemon, and orange so that it protrudes an equal distance on each side of the fruit. Bend the wires into a "U" shape toward the stem end of each piece of fruit.①

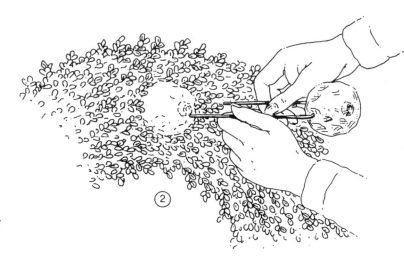

Center a pomegranate at the top of the wreath. Face the blossom end of the pomegranate outward. Attach the pomegranate to the wreath by holding the wire ends 2 inches apart and pushing them through the middle of the boxwood.② Twist the wires several times at the back of the wreath to secure the pomegranate.③ Cut off any excess wire. Center a pomegranate at each side and at the bottom of the wreath. Attach them in the same manner.

Center a lady apple above and below the

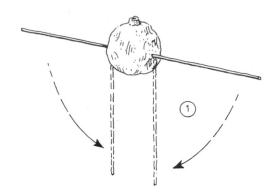

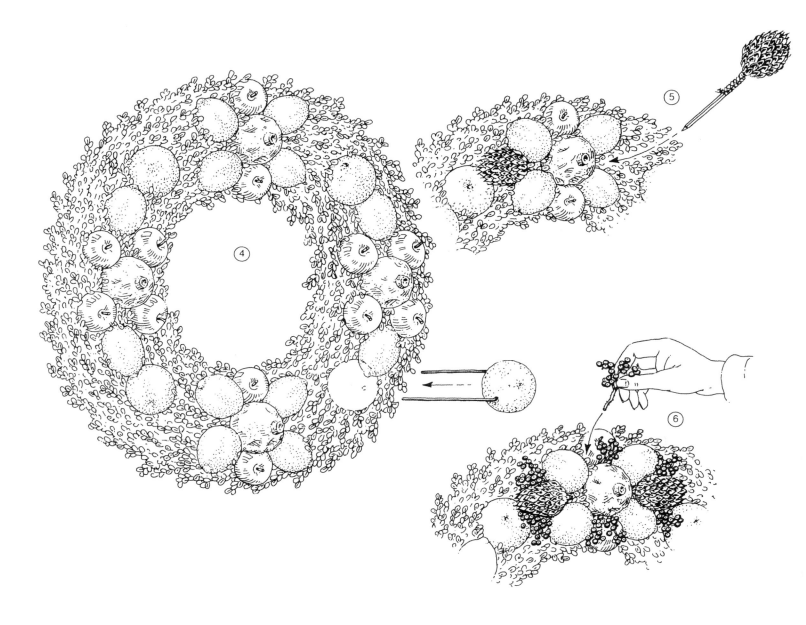

top and bottom pomegranates. Center 2 lady apples, side by side, above and below the pomegranates on each side of the wreath. Attach them in the same manner.

Position and attach 4 lemons on their sides around the pomegranate at the top of the wreath and 4 around the pomegranate at the bottom. Position and attach 1 lemon above and 1 below the lady apples on each side of the wreath.

Position and attach the 4 oranges as shown in the illustration.④

Wire the magnolia pods on 4-inch floral picks by wrapping the wire on the picks around the stems tightly several times. Bring the wire below the stem and wrap it around the floral pick only several times. Stick 1 magnolia pod to the right and 1 to the left of the top pomegranate and 2 to the left of the bottom pomegranate.⑤

Tuck the sprigs of pyracantha into the boxwood at the top and bottom of the wreath as illustrated.⑥

Apple Cone

1 cone-shaped wooden form 10 inches high,
  5 inches wide at the base, and $2^1/2$
  inches wide at the top

58 2-inch finishing nails have been driven
  into the form in 9 vertical rows with
  6 nails in each row and 4 nails in the
  top; all of the nails extend outward
  1 inch from the base (See Products List)

15 flat magnolia leaves that are uniform in size
Clippers

Flat plate or cardboard 10 inches in diameter
22 to 36 medium red Delicious apples
1 large apple for the top or 1 miniature
pineapple
4-inch sprigs of boxwood

The apple cone is one of the most popular Williamsburg table decorations. The size and shape of the apples available will determine the exact number needed. In general, the largest, fattest apples should be used on the bottom row of the cone and the thinnest apples for the most compact rows. Tucking in sprigs of boxwood to fill spaces between the fruit will greatly improve the appearance of an apple cone.

Cut off the stems and trim the bases of the magnolia leaves with the clippers.① Arrange the leaves so that they cover the plate or cardboard.② The pointed ends should extend beyond the outer edge.

Place the wooden form on top of the leaves.③

DESIGN I: Use the smaller apples for this arrangement, which has 8 apples in each of 3 rows and 1 apple on top. Starting at the bottom of the cone, impale a horizontal row of 8 of the largest apples, evenly spaced. There are 9 nails in the horizontal row, so some of the apples must be impaled off-center. Impale a second horizontal row of 8 apples directly above the first row. Impale a third horizontal row of the 8 thinnest apples directly above the first two rows. It may be necessary to rearrange the apples in the third row until they fit on the cone. Impale 1 large apple on the top nail. If the apples selected for this arrangement are quite small, 9 may be used

in the first 2 rows and 1 or 2 fewer in the third row, arranged in a pleasing way.④

DESIGN II: This arrangement is created in the same manner as Design I. It features 3 horizontal rows with 7 apples in each row and 1 large apple on top. The spaces between the apples will be wider, but they will be filled in with boxwood.⑤

DESIGN III: Starting at the bottom of the cone, impale a horizontal row of 8 of the largest apples, evenly spaced. Alternate a second horizontal row of 8 apples above the first row. Arrange a third horizontal row of 7 apples in a pleasing way to compensate for the decreasing size of the cone. Impale 1 large apple on the top nail.⑥

DESIGN IV: Starting at the bottom of the cone, impale a horizontal row of 9 of the largest apples, stems facing outward, with 1 apple on each nail. Alternate a second horizontal row of 9 apples above the first row. The apples in the second row must be impaled off-center. Alternate a third horizontal row of 9 of the thinnest apples above the second row. Arrange the fourth row of 8 apples to create a symmetrically pleasing design. Impale 1 large apple, a miniature pineapple, the top half of a large pineapple, or even pineapple foliage alone on the top nail.⑦

Tuck in sprigs of boxwood to fill spaces between the apples.

NOTE: If magnolia leaves are not available, rhododendron or other large, flat leaves may be substituted. Sprigs of holly, white pine, or other bushy foliage may be used in place of the boxwood.

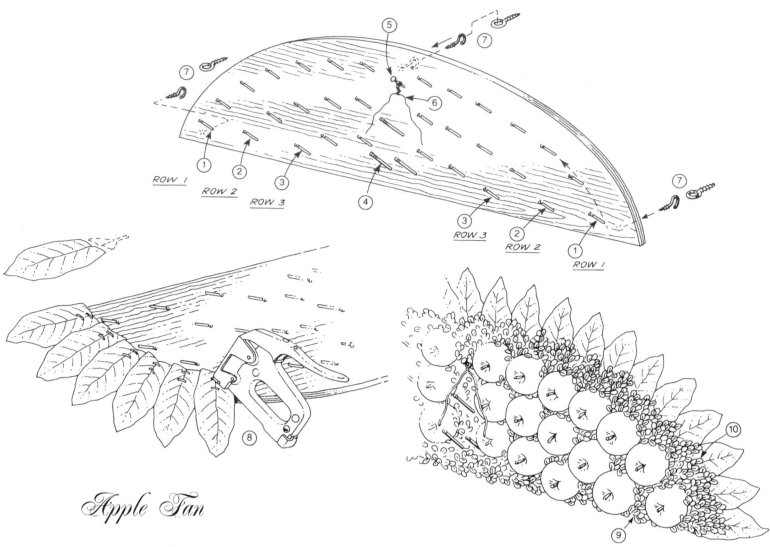

ROW 1   ROW 2   ROW 3   ROW 3   ROW 2   ROW 1

Apple Fan

1 piece of ¹/₂ inch thick plywood board cut
    into a fan shape to fit the top of the door
    frame; the board illustrated is 40 inches
    long x 12 inches high in the center
Hammer
30 eightpenny finishing nails
3 tenpenny finishing nails
1 fourpenny box nail
1 piece of #22-gauge floral wire 12 inches in
    length
3 screw hooks
3 screw eyes
Staple gun with staples
22 large magnolia leaves that are uniform
    in size
Clippers

80 3-inch sprigs of boxwood
30 large red Delicious apples
1 medium to large pineapple
3 pieces of #16-gauge floral wire in 6-inch
    lengths

Begin at the lower right corner of the frame 2¹/₂
inches from the outer edge. Drive a row of 7
eightpenny finishing nails into the board
approximately 3 inches apart along the outer
curve and ending just to the right of center.①
The row of nails should slant upward 1³/₄ inches
from the board. The center space will be filled by
the pineapple.

    Leave 4 inches between the rows of nails.
Drive in another row of 5 upward-slanting nails

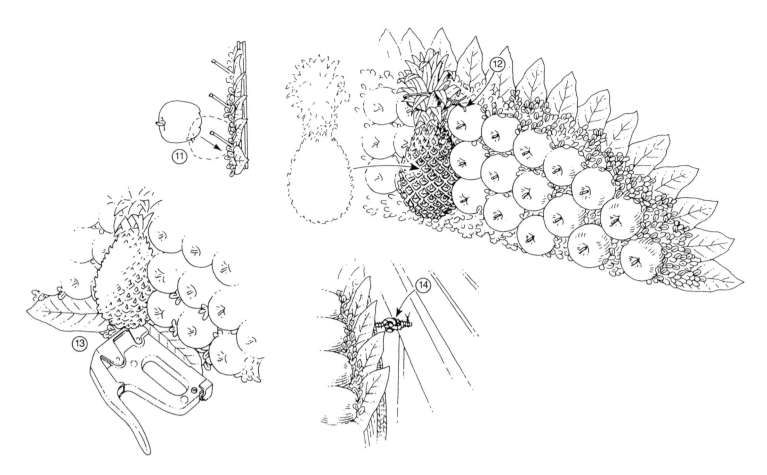

3 inches apart.② Drive in the last row of 3 upward-slanting nails 3 inches apart.③ Repeat on the left side of the frame.

Drive the 3 tenpenny nails into the center of the frame in a triangle.④ Drive the four-penny nail into the frame above the triangle 3 1/2 inches from the top center edge.⑤ Twist the piece of #22 gauge floral wire around the nail.⑥ It will be used to secure the pineapple top.

Attach a screw hook on the back of the board at the center top, 2 inches from the edge. Attach a screw hook at each corner 2 inches in from the edges.⑦ Attach corresponding screw eyes on the building.

Cut the stem ends off of 22 magnolia leaves with the clippers. Staple 20 magnolia leaves to the top curve of the board in a fan shape so that the leaves protrude outward 3 to 4 inches from the edge of the board.⑧

Staple 3-inch springs of boxwood onto the board so that it is covered.⑨ Some sprigs of boxwood should cover the stem ends of the magnolia leaves.⑩ Staple sprigs of boxwood along the edges of the board.

Impale an apple on each nail. The stem end should face outward.⑪ Impale the pineapple on the 3 nails in the center of the board. Wrap the wire through the leaves of the pineapple to secure it. Twist the wire several times in back of the pineapple foliage.⑫

Staple 2 magnolia leaves at the base of the pineapple as illustrated. The stem ends should be tucked under the pineapple.⑬

To secure the board to the building, hook the screw hooks through the screw eyes. Wrap a piece of #16-gauge floral wire around each hook and eye.⑭

Index

Acknowledgments

Many thanks to the residents of Williamsburg's Historic Area who, since 1935, have decorated their doors, windows, gates, and outbuildings with such care and creativity so that every year the decorations look better than they did the one before. Special thanks go to all who helped with the research and photography for this book, particularly Jacqueline and Benjamin White, Mary and Tom Horton, Robert Rentz, Tanya Wilson, John Gonzales, Helen Dorsey, Susan Dippre, Marion Abbitt, Donna Sheppard, Dennis Montgomery, Dave Doody, Rita Grove, Louise Kelley, Gloria McFadden, Brian Lambert, Marianne Martin, Julie Stanton, George Wilson, Dianne Spence, Wendy Howell, Emma L. Powers, Dan Hawks, Peg Smith, and the reference librarians at the Henrico County Public Library. Thanks also to our editor Howard W. Reeves and his able assistant, Lia Ronnen, at Harry N. Abrams, Inc.